3/7/21.

KT-559-166

BSRE

Please return/renew this item by the last date shown
on this label, or on your self-service receipt.

To renew this item, visit **www.librarieswest.org.uk**
or contact your library

Your borrower number and PIN are required.

Libraries**West**

www.penguin.co.uk

4 4 0059553 8

Alan Johnson was born in North Kensington in 1950. He stacked supermarket shelves whilst pursuing his big break in pop music with two local bands. A postman for twenty years, Alan rose through the ranks of the Communication Workers Union, becoming General Secretary in 1992. He was elected to Parliament as the MP for Hull West and Hessle in 1997 and served in five cabinet positions, including Home Secretary, during the Blair and Brown governments. Alan stepped down from Parliament in 2017.

His first book, *This Boy*, won the RSL Ondaatje Prize and the Orwell Prize in 2013. His second, *Please, Mister Postman*, won the National Book Award for Autobiography of the Year in 2014. His third, *The Long and Winding Road*, was published in 2016 and won the Parliamentary Book Award for Best Memoir. Alan Johnson lives in East Yorkshire and is still passionate about music.

Also by Alan Johnson

This Boy
Please, Mister Postman
The Long and Winding Road

In My Life

A Music Memoir

Alan Johnson

CORGI BOOKS

TRANSWORLD PUBLISHERS
61–63 Uxbridge Road, London W5 5SA
www.penguin.co.uk

Transworld is part of the Penguin Random House group of companies
whose addresses can be found at global.penguinrandomhouse.com

First published in Great Britain in 2018 by Bantam Press
an imprint of Transworld Publishers
Corgi edition published 2019

A CIP catalogue record for this book is available from the British Library.

ISBN
9780552174763

Typeset in 11.04/14.40pt Minion by Jouve (UK), Milton Keynes.
Printed and bound in Great Britain by Clays Ltd, Elcograf S.p.A.

Penguin Random House is committed to a sustainable
future for our business, our readers and our planet. This book
is made from Forest Stewardship Council® certified paper.

1 3 5 7 9 10 8 6 4 2

For Carolyn

Contents

CONTENTS

Introduction

A T THE BEGINNING of the century David Bowie predicted that 'music itself is going to become like running water or electricity'.

Today it seems as if Bowie's prediction has come to pass. There are numerous radio stations, as well as video channels such as MTV, pumping out pop every minute of the day and night; computers, mobile phones and laptops offer new and ever-more sophisticated access, and streaming platforms provide the facility for listeners to hear exactly what they want, when they want to hear it.

Bowie, like me, was born in the era of music famine but, unlike me, contributed to the feast that was to come.

I may not have made an impact on the music scene, but it has none the less had an enormous impact on me. This memoir traces the twenty-five years in which I believed I might be able to fulfil my dream of making my living by playing music or writing songs. Dreams differ from aspirations and ambitions in that they are rarely founded in reality, and mine proved to be unrealisable as I was never remotely good enough.

This quarter-of-a-century slice of my life follows, year by

year, the growth of pop music in tandem with my own development. It encompasses, if not the birth of rock 'n' roll, certainly its post-natal phase, the arrival of the Beatles, the band that remain as much of a music sensation today as they were sixty years ago, and the myriad artists and genres that succeeded them into the 1970s and 1980s.

I write not as a music historian but as one of the millions whose lives were enhanced by the music we loved. Born into a world before even electricity was ubiquitous, we grew up without many of the things that would today be considered basic essentials. Access to pop music was just one of them. Whether abundance has been a good or a bad thing, I'll leave the reader to decide.

1957

True Love

IT'S SUNDAY LUNCHTIME in Southam Street, London W10. In truth the word 'lunch' belonged at the posher end of Ladbroke Grove. To us this was dinnertime. If we ate anything in the evening, it was for our tea.

My father Steve had already applied silver armbands to the over-long sleeves of his newly ironed, double-cuffed shirt, polished his shoes, Brylcreemed his hair, fixed his tie, donned his suit and set off for the pub. It was like obeying a call to prayer; as if a siren had sounded at 12 noon to summon thousands of working-class men to the Sunday ritual of a lunchtime drink.

They didn't have far to go. There was a boozer on every corner, and in the corner of every boozer, a piano. (Or, in the rhyming slang that was as common in west London as it was in the East End, every battle cruiser had a joanna.) On the corner of Southam Street was the Earl of Warwick, in the next street, the Derby Arms and on Middle Row, a five-minute walk away, the Lads of the Village, which was Steve's destination. As a pub pianist, he was well known in the haunts of North Kensington. His wife, my mother

Lily, like almost all the women, stayed at home to cook the Sunday roast, which had to be on the table at 2pm when, with a bit of luck, her husband would return.

Steve had already failed to return once. In 1953 he had gone off with the wife of his best friend, only to return six months later having fathered a half-brother I've never met. It would only be a matter of time before he left for good. His sole legacy to my older sister Linda and me would be his honky-tonk piano and a love of music that was deeply embedded in our DNA. For now, the piano was out of bounds. He kept the keyboard locked to prevent us from experimenting with it.

Linda and I, aged ten and seven respectively, would be contemplating the endless, enervating day that lay ahead. Sunday was a day of rituals. For some this may have included a church service but ours was not a churchgoing community. There were many more pubs than churches and my mother, while a firm believer, never worshipped in the conventional way.

Her relationship with God seemed more personal and intimate. When the gas meter required feeding, for instance, and she'd managed to unearth a shilling from somewhere, she would lift her face towards the heavens, which lay somewhere above our fly-infested ceiling, and, her eyes tightly shut, whisper a prayer of thanks.

Inside the meter was a wheel that could be seen turning, indicating the speed at which your shilling pieces were being devoured. By around 1.30 on Sundays, that wheel would be spinning like a top as Lily roasted the meat, over-boiled the veg and baked the bread pudding ahead of the 2pm deadline.

The enormous wireless, hired from Radio Rentals, would be tuned to the BBC Light Programme as, I suspect, was almost every other radio in the country. There was no alternative to the BBC in 1957. Commercial radio was years away and while the names of overseas stations such as Luxembourg and Hilversum were optimistically printed on to some tuning dials, getting any reception through the maze of atmospheric noise was difficult.

Our radio didn't offer even the remote hope of such exotic alternatives. The Radio Rentals engineer had installed it high up, its wires running into a brown Bakelite casing fixed to the kitchen door frame at eye level. This provided us with a switch and three numbers. The choice was 1 for the Light Programme, 2 for the Home Service, which broadcast mainly news and current affairs, and 3 for the classical music offered by the Third Programme.

At that particular time on a Sunday most of the nation was tuned to *Two-Way Family Favourites* on the Light Programme. There were four or five families in every house in Southam Street, some packed into single rooms, others, like us, progressing to two or three rooms split between landings. From every radio came the same opening theme tune: the lush strings of the Andre Kostelanetz Orchestra playing 'With a Song in My Heart'. It seeped out of every cracked window and from under every misaligned door.

As the men returned from the pub at closing time the mean air of Kensal Town would be scented with the smell of roasting meat. Steve rarely returned with a song in his heart and when he did it soon gave way to the beer in his belly. He would become morose and occasionally violent.

For my mother those two hours on a Sunday lunchtime listening to *Family Favourites* provided a serene interlude.

The programme, like its forerunner, *Forces Favourites*, was a request show devised to connect those serving with the forces in West Germany and across the Commonwealth with their families back in the UK. But because it was one of the few radio programmes devoted exclusively to playing actual records, as opposed to broadcasting renditions of popular songs played in a studio by one of the BBC's in-house orchestras, it attracted massive audiences from all walks of life, at its peak reaching 26 million.

Jean Metcalfe hosted the show from London, with links to a variety of announcers based at BFPO (British Forces Posted Overseas) stations in Germany and farther-flung locations. One of them was her husband, Cliff Michelmore, whom she'd 'met' through the programme when he co-presented it from Hamburg (apparently, he used to say it had been 'love at first hearing'), though at the time it was considered unseemly for that secret to be shared with listeners. The announcers would take turns to read out dedications and requests from soldiers to their families at home and from families to the soldiers stationed abroad. The highlight of the show was when the 'Bumper Bundle' (the song that had been requested in more letters than any other) was revealed.

In 1957, the Bumper Bundle was, more often than not, 'True Love' by Bing Crosby and Grace Kelly, released the previous year. In my mind's eye, when this comes on the radio I am playing with some toys on the kitchen lino and look up at my pretty Scouse mother as she rushes in from the gas cooker on the landing and sinks her tiny frame into a battered chair, dishcloth in hand and a faraway look in her eye, to listen to Bing and Grace croon her favourite tune.

Still a young woman, Lily generally keeps her chestnut hair

pinned, clipped and gripped beneath a turban, as it is now. The turban is only discarded when she gets dolled up for 'the pictures', her weekly escape alone to the Odeon or the Royalty to see Cary Grant, Doris Day or Gary Cooper. It is as if the glamour on the screen demands an equivalent dress code on the part of the audience.

Grace Kelly is her favourite film star, as she never fails to remind my sister and me when 'True Love' begins to play and we are shushed into silence. I, too, am keen to listen. I like the wistful melody of Cole Porter's song and the harmony near the end, which appears to be Grace's only contribution.

Nevertheless she shared the credits with Bing, and thus, I discovered when I was a bit older and obsessed with the 'hit parade', added a number 4 hit in the UK charts and a gold record to her already impressive CV in the year she married Prince Rainier of Monaco and became a princess.

The film in which the record featured, *High Society*, starring Bing and Grace alongside Frank Sinatra, had also been released in 1956. Lily told us she loved that film so much she'd stayed in the cinema to watch it a second time. Having paid the admission charge, picturegoers could, and often did, remain in the warm, dark comfort of the cinema for as many screenings as they liked.

'For you and I have a guardian angel on high with nothing to do,' Bing and Grace sang. A guardian angel for Lily would certainly not have been under-occupied. Her hard life was soon to become much harder as her health deteriorated and she struggled to cope without her feckless husband.

'True Love' would go on to be covered by a disparate collection of artists – among them Richard Chamberlain, Frank Sinatra's daughter Nancy, Shakin' Stevens and Elton John and

Kiki Dee. There was even a blues version by George Harrison. But for me none carries the poignancy brought to the song by Bing and Grace in my childhood.

As the last notes of 'True Love' faded on a Sunday dinner-time, Lily would return to reality. The meal would be eaten in silence and the rest of the day would be passed in a kind of stupor. We had no television to watch. Lily had taught us card games such as kings, rummy and whist, but in working-class households, at least, irrespective of their level of religious observance, playing cards was banned on Sunday. It wasn't so many years since 'noisy jazz' had been forbidden on the Sabbath even on *Two-Way Family Favourites*. We were condemned to silence as Steve, stretched out on the old mock leather armchair which nobody else was allowed to occupy, snored his way through the endless afternoon.

1958

Tom Dooley

REFLECTING ON MY childhood memoir *This Boy*, a radio interviewer described music as our escape from the slums. I never saw it that way. For a start, I wasn't ever aware that I was living in a slum and had no conception of what life might be like elsewhere. Everyone around us lived in the same conditions. What was there to escape from, and where would we escape to?

If our mother's cleaning jobs in the more prosperous households of Notting Hill and South Kensington gave us the odd glimpse of another kind of existence, we never saw it as part of our world. For all we had in common with these families, we might as well have arrived from another planet. We understood instinctively that the lives they led were completely different from ours and it never occurred to us to resent their obvious affluence. More often than not, when Lily was obliged to take us with her during the school holidays, we'd be dispatched to Kensington Gardens for the day, where Linda was deputed to watch over me while our mother completed her roster of dusting and polishing, sweeping and scrubbing. That was fine by us. We loved Kensington Gardens and we'd have been uncomfortable, not to say bored stiff, if forced to sit indoors in such alien territory.

I remember our mother telling us that the children in one of these families had been sent away to boarding school. Linda and I were horrified. We couldn't imagine any greater deprivation. If those same 'privileged' children, living at the posh end of the Royal Borough of Kensington, were as beguiled by music as we were, it wouldn't be seen as an 'escape' from their life, but as an integral part of it. And so it was for us.

There wasn't much else to distract us. As far as we knew, nobody in Southam Street had a television set. Linda's friend Marilyn Hughes, who lived a few streets away, was the only child we knew whose family possessed a television. By 1958, we had no TV and no father. If we we regretted one of these privations, it was the telly rather than the dad.

Our father eloped one Saturday morning with the barmaid from the Lads of the Village, leaving his wife distraught and his children happy. We couldn't understand why our mother was so upset. Linda knew more than I did about our father's antics. She knew that he contributed nothing to our upkeep apart from the coins Lily managed to filch from the bedside where he'd empty his pockets at night before falling into a drunken stupor. He rarely plied his trade as a painter and decorator, preferring his other, twilight occupation as musician, gambler and 'ladies' man'. The daily grind of earning a living was left to Lily. Worst of all, when he came home drunk he'd beat her. While she could give as good as she got in a verbal exchange, there was little she could do to counter his slaps and punches.

In the end he'd gone quietly, creeping away while the three of us were in the Portobello Road looking for second-hand clothes 'off the barrow'. We'd returned home to find we'd become a single-parent family. What Linda and I failed to understand, as our mother sat quietly sobbing at the blue Formica kitchen table, twisting a tear-drenched handkerchief round and round her fingers, was that this wasn't the end of the hard times. For Lily in particular, it was the beginning of a new and darker chapter.

For a start, she was lonely, and would now be even lonelier. She had become an abandoned woman and somehow, in our neighbourhood, abandonment was always the woman's fault. But there would also be practical difficulties. Back then a married woman couldn't sign a hire-purchase agreement or rent a telly without her husband being present to countersign the paperwork. Worst of all, she had no idea where Steve had gone, and to pursue a maintenance claim through the courts she would have to track him down. In the meantime we'd be poorer than ever because the family allowance to which we were entitled was paid to him, not to her. For women this was the post-emancipation, pre-equal-opportunities period of British social history.

And yes, undoubtedly those tears fell more heavily because, despite everything, Lily still loved Steve and had lost him to another woman.

～

The musical accompaniment to Lily's consternation and our relief was provided by Lonnie Donegan and Cliff Richard.

Linda had a pre-pubescent crush on Cliff. The dark, bequiffed lad from Cheshunt was basically an Elvis Presley tribute act, as were most British pop stars of that era.

The first homegrown answer to Elvis, an ex-Merchant Navy seaman called Tommy Steele, had been launched on to the music scene in 1956. He opened the door to a plethora of British rockers with edgy stage names like Power, Wilde and Fury.

I considered Lonnie, my favourite, to be more authentic than Cliff or Marty Wilde (born Reginald Smith in Blackheath) or Adam Faith, from just down the road in Acton. For a start he actually played the guitar the others would occasionally sling round their necks for adornment. His first hit, 'Rock Island Line', had been written by the great African-American folk singer Leadbelly, who served time in the Louisiana state penitentiary for attempted murder, and at the end of 1958, the year he permeated my eight-year-old consciousness, Lonnie was in the charts with a version of an old folk song of the American south that seemed to me to be more profound than the 'moon in June' ditties warbled by the others. As can be seen, I suffered from early onset pretentiousness.

That year poor, struggling, worn-out Lily somehow managed to ensure that both of her children got to see their musical heroes. She entered Linda for a competition in the *London Evening News* to try to win tickets for a Cliff Richard concert at the London Palladium. To the disbelief and delight of all three of us, Linda landed an allocated seat at this famous venue for a Sunday matinee performance.

Lily and I accompanied her as far as the theatre, just off Regent Street, where my sister joined hundreds of other girls and their parents milling about waiting for the doors to open.

The excitement in the air was palpable. Then we had to wait until the show was over to see her safely home again, which meant hanging around an otherwise deserted Sunday afternoon West End for several hours, trudging past endless parades of closed shops. On the plus side, I saw the statue of Eros at Piccadilly Circus for the first time and, at Portland Place at the other end of Regent Street, Broadcasting House, the art-deco structure from which emanated that cornucopia of entertainment accessed through our three-channel Bakelite switch. From there we returned to the Palladium just as Linda emerged, breathless after screaming for two hours at the object of her adoration.

Towards the end of the year my mother took me to the Chiswick Empire, where Lonnie Donegan was appearing. Linda had seen her hero and now I must see mine. It was just the two of us, Lily and me. Lily applied her deep red lipstick, pinned her hair into its 'going out' mode, the style she wore when she went to the pictures, and we took the bus to Chiswick High Road. It was one of those wet winter evenings that pervade my childhood memories, the deep yellow street lights reflecting off the damp pavements like pools of melting lemons as men strode along, hat brims pulled down and the lapels of their gabardine macs turned up against the grey drizzle.

As it was close to Christmas, I've always had the event filed in my memory as a pantomime, but I think it must have been a variety show of the kind that still packed theatres across the country into the 1960s, which usually featured a magician, a comedian and a troupe of tumbling acrobats as well as the musical acts. I can't remember any of those, or indeed anything else from the show apart from the man I'd come to see. I do recall that Lonnie and his six-piece band weren't actually top of the bill: that distinction fell to Joan Regan, a blonde singer, one of a legion of British crooners – David Whitfield, Ruby Murray, Dickie Valentine, Lita Roza, Dennis Lotis, Alma Cogan – who were soon destined for extinction in the evolutionary process that was changing popular music.

I was lucky to have the chance to soak up the atmosphere of the Chiswick Empire when I did because the following summer it was abruptly closed after the building was sold and plans approved for a lucrative office block. It seems the news came as a bombshell to the staff: the theatre played to capacity audiences, and in what turned out to be its last show, the flamboyant pianist Liberace wowed a full house.

In fact, Lonnie Donegan had been in pantomime at the Chiswick Empire the previous year, in the first of many panto appearances (giving his Wishee-Washee in *Aladdin*), derided by purists as 'selling out'. No doubt to an experienced artist like Lonnie, who had been performing since the 1940s, it was just another paying job. But it is perhaps ironic that he began to broaden into an old-fashioned, all-round entertainer just as the musical revolution he had helped to create was about to consign that particular breed to history.

Lonnie would very soon develop a repertoire that wouldn't have been out of place in a Victorian music hall – songs like 'My Old Man's a Dustman' and 'Does Your Chewing Gum Lose Its Flavour on the Bedpost Overnight' – which would dent his credibility among his teenage audience. Yet he and the skiffle genre he popularised, a blend of jazz, blues and folk often played on improvised instruments, was probably responsible for more young boys picking up a guitar and learning how to play it (or even a washboard or comb and paper) than any-one other than Bert Weedon, of *Play in a Day* fame. It would not be a stretch to describe Lonnie as the architect of the 1960s pop explosion.

In the winter of 1958, I sat in the binding darkness of the stalls waiting patiently for the penultimate act. I was enthralled by the whole experience of seeing Lonnie live on stage, of shar-ing the air he breathed, marvelling that he was occupying the same moment in time and space as me – and my mum. I suspect that Lily was only pretending to enjoy Lonnie's performance out of loyalty to her son. She'd have been looking forward to Joan Regan. There was nothing about skiffle or rock 'n' roll that moved my mother one iota. The only 'group' that she ever liked was the Bachelors, and they were to rock 'n' roll what Jerry Lee Lewis was to Beethoven's sonatas.

That evening Lonnie was not singing about chewing gum or dustmen but about being one of them rambling men; about the big Columbia River and the big Grand Coulee Dam. There was pathos, history, drama; there were catchy choruses, and virtu-oso instrumentals. And, of course, he sang about Tom Dooley, the poor boy who was bound to die – the hit that was Number 3 in the charts at the time and one of the Top 20 bestselling singles of the whole year, in spite of having to compete with a rival recording of the same song from across the Atlantic by the Kingston Trio.

He was, in short, singing in American. And everything to do with the best entertainment came from the States. As Cliff and his fellow Elvis impersonators were carving out their careers in British pop, their established equivalents, the home-grown crooners, were still imitating their US idols, Frank Sinatra, Mel

Tormé and Rosemary Clooney. The best films came from Hollywood and the TV schedules were saturated with westerns – *The Cisco Kid, Gun Law, The Lone Ranger, Cheyenne, Laramie.*

Lonnie's assimilation of the American experience was part of his appeal for me. My passion for music was fuelled by those TV cowboy heroes long before we acquired our first television. I sat spellbound as the radio played Frankie Laine singing 'Do Not Forsake Me, O My Darlin'', the haunting theme from the film *High Noon.* Its sombre minor key sent shivers down my spine and I thought it was the most exciting song I'd ever heard. It inspired me to write my own western ballad, 'As the Wagons Keep on Rollin'' (Through this dark and barren land/The Indians are waiting to get your cowhand/They'll be burning every wagon and killin' every man/I don't think anyone can get through/I'd be surprised if anyone can'). I sang this potential classic to my mother, accompanying myself on my plastic 'Tommy Steele' guitar. Just the once. There were no demands for an encore.

I liked the drama of the cowboy songs, their dark themes and rousing choruses. I didn't know the genre as country and western, but that's what it was. And prominent in the musical accompaniment was my instrument of choice: the guitar.

At school my sister and I played the descant recorder, as every child was obliged to do at the time. Linda also had a Melodica, given to her as a Christmas present. These plastic wind instruments with two-octave piano keyboards were expected to catch on in a big way but never really did. We also now had access to our father's honky-tonk piano, one of Linda's first acts as we celebrated his departure having been to break the lock with a screwdriver and liberate the keys. But for me none of these instruments could match the guitar.

My mother had bought me that toy 'Tommy Steele' guitar as a birthday present one year. Small and brittle, it had four thick, plastic strings in primary colours – one red, one yellow, one blue and one green – and plonked rather than strummed. It was upgraded to a proper six-string Spanish guitar, thanks to her win on the football pools, in 1957. The windfall wasn't a life-changing sum – about £90 – but one which in those days was enough to put down deposits on various household items she could previously only dream of owning. But the money didn't last long, especially after Steve got his hands on some of it and proceeded to gamble it away, and most of her acquisitions were soon either returned or repossessed because she couldn't afford the repayments.

In truth, the three-piece suite, sideboard and new kitchen table that came and went had looked a bit incongruous in our Southam Street rooms. The suite had to be stored in the bedroom as we didn't have a front room to put it in.

The two purchases that survived were my Spanish guitar and the Dansette record-player that represented Linda's share of our mother's good fortune.

The guitar wasn't an expensive one, but I was thrilled with it. Lily helped me to pick it out of a mail-order catalogue, placing a strict limit on the cost. It had the appropriate burnished-wood body, six metal strings and a plastic scratchboard located just under the sound hole. Its smell of wood and polish and varnish has stayed with me down the years, reminding me of one of the most joyful days of my life – the day that guitar first arrived. It was almost as long as me, a full-sized instrument. And it looked just like Lonnie's.

1959

It Doesn't Matter Anymore

W E ALL HAVE distinct scraps of memory, like video clips we replay in our minds; a record of a time and place, sometimes enhanced by sounds and smells, that remains indelible as other recollections fade. I have many in my mental library. One of the clearest dates from the summer of 1959.

The weather is hot and clammy. The big window in the bedroom I still share with my sister has been raised on its threadbare sash and is suspended like a guillotine above my head while I gaze out on the street below. Southam Street is teeming as the long summer evening unfurls, the heat compounding the effects of the poor sanitation to drive people out of doors.

Linda is out somewhere, probably at the Girl Guides, where she was an enthusiastic pack leader. She acquired many badges demonstrating her proficiency in a variety of essential skills such as chopping wood and making a fire, each sewn carefully on to the sleeve of her blue Guide's blouse. And she learned lots of songs, which she insisted on singing to me. Most, like the archetypal 'Ging Gang Goolie', were innocent gibberish, but I recall another, which must have been sung when Brown Owl, or whatever the head Guide was called, wasn't around. I can't remember it all, but the first line was: 'On top of Old Smokey where nobody goes, there stands Jayne Mansfield without any clothes.'

Anyway, my sister isn't around and I'm leaning on a flaked and crumbling windowsill that forms the only barrier between me and the 30ft drop into the 'area' below (or the 'airie', as we kids called it). My mother joins me, bringing an old pillow to protect our bare arms from the rough edges as we lean out together to catch whatever breeze may be drifting past and to see what is happening down towards Golborne Road. It is not long after the Whitsun bank holiday Monday when, right there, at the corner of our street, Kelso Cochrane, a young Antiguan carpenter, was murdered by a gang of Teddy Boys.

Although all seems peaceful, and the few West Indian residents of Southam Street, who live at the other end, tend to keep themselves to themselves for fear of attracting any unwanted scrutiny, there is an undercurrent of tension in the oppressive heat. The senseless killing of Kelso Cochrane has brought a lot of attention to our previously largely ignored community: police conducting door-to-door inquiries, journalists seeking background, and camera crews from around Britain and abroad.

My mother had been wanting for years to move out of Southam Street, which had been declared unfit for human habitation in the 1930s, and this shocking event only sharpened her desire to escape. But the council house waiting list was long and our housing provider, the Rowe Housing Trust, was still trying to find us somewhere else to live; a place where Linda, who would be twelve in September, would no longer have to share a bedroom with her kid brother.

In the meantime, Lily had picked up an old folding screen from somewhere, the kind that doctors had in their surgeries, behind which patients would be invited to step to remove their clothing. This was strategically positioned in the space between our beds to provide some rudimentary privacy, particularly when we had to pee in a bucket during the night. It was that or go down three flights of stairs wearing makeshift nightclothes in the pitch dark to use the decrepit toilet in the back yard.

I was very prudish about being seen in a state of undress. It was certainly a more modest age. But, thinking back, I suspect I suffered from a mild form of what we now know as obsessive-compulsive disorder (OCD), because I definitely had some peculiar bedtime rituals. The main one was centred on a girl named Jennifer Shepherd, who was in my class at Bevington Primary School and lived further down Southam Street. Every night as I undressed behind the screen, before I took my trousers off, I would check under the bed in case Jennifer was hiding there. I was not concerned that Josie Rose or Maureen Langton or Norma Dixon or any of the other girls in my class might have secreted themselves beneath the bed – no, this was a specific search for Jennifer Shepherd. Exactly what the poor girl had done to deserve this role as the object of my strange obsession I haven't the faintest idea.

It was certainly not illogical to think that somebody could have sneaked into our room, even if it was highly unlikely to have been Jennifer Shepherd. None of the doors had locks, and while we had the upstairs floor to ourselves, with its two rooms and the cooker out on the landing, on the next floor down, where Linda and I slept, there was another family packed into the room opposite. Nothing other than an inbred sense of decorum among the occupants and boundaries that existed only in our imaginations prevented cross-pollination between the four or five different families who filled the house. Once through the front door on some pretence or other, a visitor or intruder could have entered any room at random.

As things turned out, this would be our last summer in Southam Street. And on this evening, as Lily and I take the air from our elevated vantage point, surveying the bustle on the pavement below, there is a song playing on a radio somewhere, the volume amplified through an open window. It is Buddy Holly singing 'It Doesn't Matter Anymore'.

Buddy was everywhere that year. His death in a plane crash in February at the tender age of twenty-two had sealed his immortality, and that single carried a particular sorrowful piquancy, having been released posthumously.

As a nine-year-old obsessed with pop music, I followed the charts diligently and listened avidly to the few record shows offered by the BBC. There was *Housewives Choice*, more Perry Como and Lena Horne than rock 'n' roll, Sam Costa, and *Children's Favourites*, introduced by 'Uncle Mac' with the greeting 'Hello, children everywhere!'. But I was outgrowing 'Nellie the Elephant', 'Sparky's Magic Piano' and Danny Kaye's glorious rendition of 'The Ugly Duckling'. I wanted to hear Neil Sedaka, Jerry Keller's 'Here Comes Summer', Marty Robbins and, of course, Lonnie Donegan. So the highlights of my week were the BBC's chart programme, *Pick of the Pops*, with David Jacobs, and *Record Roundup*, hosted by Jack Jackson, a former bandleader and trumpeter. He pioneered the use of comedy clips and pre-recorded tapes between records adopted by later disc jockeys like Kenny Everett and Noel Edmonds.

As a child, of course, I just accepted the scarcity of records on the BBC as a fact of life. The reason for it was a precedent set by an agreement with the Musicians' Union dating back to 1934, which imposed 'needle time' restrictions on the corporation. In the 1950s, the playing of commercial gramophone records was limited to under thirty hours a week. All other music had to be 'live'. This had never been much of an issue while listeners preferred live dance-band music to records, but now young people wanted to hear pop singles. It was a problem for the BBC that was exacerbated by the cost of using live music at a time when resources were increasingly being diverted from radio to television.

Whatever airwaves were available to original pop recordings that summer, Buddy Holly dominated them, as is so often the case when the life of an artist is cut tragically short. For years after his death, Buddy's previously unreleased (and, in the later stages, 'should never have been released') material would sell much better in Britain than the records produced while he was alive ever had. And his premature demise would eventually be commemorated as 'the day the music died' in Don McLean's 'American Pie'.

I had never heard of Buddy Holly in his lifetime and quickly grew tired of 'It Doesn't Matter Anymore'. But songs such as 'Peggy Sue' and 'That'll Be the Day', coupled with the morbid fascination of the terrible plane crash that killed him, soon made me a Buddy fan.

Two other young stars, the Big Bopper (aged twenty-eight) and Ritchie Valens, of 'La Bamba' fame, who was just seventeen, perished along with Buddy and the pilot that February, minutes after taking off in snowy conditions. They had been leaving Clear Lake, Iowa, bound for Fargo, Minnesota (even the place names were redolent of the inhospitable, wide-open spaces depicted in westerns) and the next gig of a 'Winter Dance Party' tour.

It seemed to me that travelling by aeroplane in winter was suicidal. Matt Busby's brilliant Manchester United football team had also been destroyed in a disaster at Munich airport only a year, almost to the day, before Buddy's untimely death. I was crazy about football and fixated on United's goalkeeper, Harry Gregg, who had not only survived but proved himself a hero by helping to rescue other passengers, including his team-mate Bobby Charlton and manager Matt Busby, from the burning plane. Like all goalies at the time he used to play in a thick green woollen roll-neck jumper and a flat cap to keep the sun out of his eyes. I'd pretend to be Harry, throwing myself towards an imaginary shot, safe in the assurance of a soft landing on my bed.

Incredibly, Gregg returned for United's first match after the disaster, and played in every game for the remainder of the season. I was a devoted Queens Park Rangers fan but, like most of the nation, I had willed United to win the 1958 FA Cup with the motley crew of players they'd assembled post-Munich. I listened to the final on the radio and was outraged when Gregg was barged over the line along with the ball by Nat Lofthouse for Bolton's second goal.

For Linda and me the dangers of air travel were more or less on a par with the hazards of underwater exploration: we knew that there were people who experienced those risks but the chances of us being among them were so remote that the notion we might ever face such perils ourselves was hardly worth a passing thought. Our mother had never gone abroad in her life and the likelihood was that neither would we.

After an hour or so leaning on the windowsill with no sign of any tensions in the street boiling over in the heat, Lily suggests we walk round to one of the nearby corner shops that still proliferate for a packet of cigarettes. She buys them in fives, then cuts them in half with an old razor blade to give herself ten smokes, which will last her a couple of days. I am persuaded to accompany her by the promise of a Jubbly, an orange tetrahedron-shaped iced lolly – well, just a frozen drink, really – that has to be squeezed gradually out of one snipped end of its waxed cardboard cover.

As we stroll back through the syrupy air, the light is beginning to fade, and with it fades the film clip in my mind of the summer of '59. This would have been one of the last times I walked the pavements of the familiar territory into which I had been born. These North Kensington streets would soon be gone, to be replaced in part by high-rise blocks like Trellick Tower, such a potent symbol of its era that it has often featured in films, TV ads and music videos, which still marks the spot where the eastern end of our road used to be. The innocent fifties were giving way to the swinging sixties.

1960

Shakin' All Over

MINE IS A privileged generation. Not only have we prospered from the postwar rise in living standards, the creation of the NHS, significant advances in science and technology, the virtual eradication of diseases such as polio and diphtheria and the absence of world wars, we have also witnessed a transformation in public attitudes away from the casual barbarity of previous decades towards ethnic minorities, the disabled, the mentally ill, homosexuals and single mothers. Ironically, as the country has become less Christian in its adherence to religion, it has become more Christian in its way of life.

I am one of those millions of baby-boomers who began their lives in the kind of bleak slum conditions that would have been entirely familiar to Charles Dickens and will end them in a society where the absence of a second indoor toilet is considered to be a form of deprivation.

In the musical sphere, too, I feel like an archaeologist with the good fortune not only to have been present at the dawn of a new age but to have experience of an era predating my own birth. For Linda and me, this unique insight was brought about completely by happenstance.

One Saturday in the mid-1950s, our father had come home carrying on his shoulder a huge cardboard box he'd lugged back from the Portobello Road market. It contained dozens of old 78rpm records, big heavy shellac discs, each as brittle as a biscuit. A stallholder had sold him the job lot for a pound.

These relics were mainly from the 1930s, although there were a few from the 1940s and even one or two from the 1920s. Having brought them into a home with no gramophone, Steve, unusually for him, seemed content to entrust this bonanza to his children to be properly cherished as silent artefacts in their own right, which they duly were.

Cherish was the only thing we could do with them until Lily's pools win brought the Dansette into our lives. So at first, we took great delight in simply curating our collection. After we had carefully read all the labels, I was deputed by Linda to catalogue the records, noting title and artist in a ragged exercise book she'd purloined from school. She took charge of polishing them with an old rag and storing them neatly in the box in which they'd arrived. Most still had their original paper dust sleeves.

I remember the titles to this day. Our record library boasted, among other gems, 'Isle of Capri' by Ray Noble and his Orchestra, 'In a Shady Nook by a Babbling Brook' by Donald Peers and 'You're Driving Me Crazy' by Guy Lombardo and his Royal Canadians. The two I treasured the most (when I eventually got to hear them) were 'Was It Tears That Fell or Was It Rain?' by the Street Singer (Arthur Tracy), and 'With Her Head Tucked Underneath Her Arm' by Cyril Smith.

Most of the older records had an orchestral introduction

that went on for ages before an unacknowledged male vocalist with frightfully correct pronunciation came in near the end with a sprightly lyric. A good example was 'Tap Your Feet' by Jack Hylton and His Orchestra. There was no clue on the His Master's Voice record label as to who was singing it. Just the famous HMV logo, the picture of a dog with its ear to a wind-up gramophone, and beneath that image the simple phrase 'With Vocal Refrain' in brackets after the title.

An exception was the 1931 recording of 'All of Me' by Paul Whiteman, on which the celebrated Native American jazz singer Mildred Bailey was extended the courtesy of a credit for her 'Vocal Refrain'. Her name would have meant nothing to Linda and me, but it was at least preserved for posterity, unlike those of her fellow artists.

The acquisition of the record-player finally brought these relics to life, and for a good while after its arrival at Southam Street, this task was all that was asked of it. The last few years of the fifties were not an era of instant gratification for anybody, and for our mother they were particularly tough as she toiled to clothe and feed us. There was no money left for the 45rpm singles we so craved. Linda's friend Marilyn Hughes lent us some on the odd occasion, but for most of our pre-vinyl days, the beautiful red and grey Dansette was ignominiously restricted to playing music created for its wind-up ancestors.

Thankfully it had the capability to do so. There was a dial next to the turntable with three revs-per-minute settings – 33⅓, 45 and 78. The first was for vinyl long-players, the second for vinyl singles and the 78 setting was offered for those sad strangers to modernity who still retained a stake in shellac.

One of our innocent sources of amusement was to play 45s,

when we finally got them, at the lowest speed to turn them into sinister dirges, or at 78rpm so that every song sounded as if had been recorded by Pinky and Perky, two porcine string puppets who, improbable as it may seem, sang their high-pitched way to chart success in the late fifties and early sixties. As well as hosting their own TV show, they released a string of cover versions of hits of the day, including (unforgivably, as far as I was concerned) 'Tom Dooley'. The similarity was hardly surprising, as apparently this was indeed the secret to Pinky and Perky's winning formula: it was achieved by simply replaying original voice recordings, laid down on a half-speed backing track, at twice the normal speed. The only possible point of putting any of their dreadful records on the turntable would have been to listen to them at 33⅓ to hear the real, non-piggy voices.

I always thought of that Dansette as 'our' record-player even though it actually belonged to Linda. Her lack of personal space at Southam Street prevented it from being perceived as anything other than a shared resource. It was originally placed in the gap between our beds, where the modesty screen went up at night-time, this being the only position from which it could be plugged in.

Electricity had come late to Southam Street. I lived my first five years by gaslight. When 'electric' was eventually installed, it was for lighting only. The cooker used gas and the radio had been hard-wired into its own electricity supply by Radio Rentals so that it wasn't portable enough to be nicked. The romantic notion that we slum-dwellers were considered poor but honest was rather spoiled by the variety of anti-theft devices ranged against us – even the vinegar bottles in the fish-and-chip shops were chained to the counter.

Our rooms had no sockets for three-point plugs and no real need for them anyway, since none of us had washing machines, refrigerators or vacuum cleaners. So the record-player had to be connected to the electricity supply via the light fitting.

This involved Linda standing on a chair and stretching up to remove the light bulb, handing it carefully to me, and then connecting the plug on the Dansette to an adaptor that could be accommodated by the light socket. So our access to the music we craved was available only in daylight hours and therefore severely limited during the winter.

Happily, electricity sockets were provided in the four rooms at Walmer Road that the Rowe Housing Trust had found for us. By 1960 the three of us, Lily, Linda and I, had settled into our new home, where Linda and the Dansette initially had their own room, until my sister announced that she wanted us to have a 'front room' like her friends at Fulham County Grammar School. She would convert her front downstairs bedroom to this purpose and share the big double bed upstairs with our mother. As was the case with all my sister's proclamations, compliance was compulsory.

This was only part of the reason for Linda's sacrifice. Nights were an ordeal for Lily. All her worries, including her anxiety about the serious heart condition from which she suffered, came looming out of the shadows as the lights went out, and for us the sound of her sobbing had become as much a feature of the hours of darkness as the passage of the moon. Linda knew her presence would be a comfort.

Lily's token protests failed to mask her delight at this new arrangement. Furnished with Steve's battered piano and a second-hand three-piece suite upholstered in brown plastic, acquired by Lily from the Salvation Army, the 'parlour', as she took to calling it, became home to the Dansette. Freed from its dependence on the light fitting, it took pride of place, dominating the room from its perch on a built-in cupboard. Not long afterwards it was joined by our first television, hired, like the radio, from Radio Rentals.

With Linda adding a second evening job, at a chemist's in Ladbroke Grove, to the two evenings and weekends she already worked at Berriman's, the corner shop at the end of our terrace in Walmer Road, at some point in 1960 she managed to save enough to buy our first records. It took a while: the kindly Mr Berriman had initially agreed to employ Linda to enable her to pay off the bill Lily had built up by purchasing items 'on tick', so that debt had to be taken care of first. It's astonishing to think now that my redoubtable sister was still only twelve years old.

Oh, the raw excitement of the day we finally headed for the record shop 'down the Lane' (the Portobello Road). We had ten shillings, enough for two singles. Lily had topped up Linda's kitty with a couple of bob from the fluctuating maintenance payments she'd begun to receive from Steve – after she finally managed to find out where he was living and get a maintenance order made against him.

There was one unfortunate consequence to this largesse. It gave Lily a legitimate say in what we bought. That, surely, can be the only feasible explanation for how two music-savvy kids – kids who could sing 'Cathy's Clown' a cappella in perfect two-part harmony, who loved the big guitar instrumentals of the Ventures and Duane Eddy, who had looked forward for so long to owning records by Neil Sedaka and Johnny Burnette and the other US pop stars we admired – how two such cool, hip kids, with a whole record shop to choose from, could have made the selections we did. Namely 'Fings Ain't What They Used T'Be' by Max Bygraves and 'Theme from a Summer Place' by the Percy Faith Orchestra, two recordings that wouldn't have been out of place in our box of dusty 78s.

I can only hold my hand up to it, blame my mother and move on swiftly to the records that followed, as Linda scraped together enough to cough up for a single every three or four weeks. Wonderful songs by Fats Domino, Freddy Cannon, Connie Francis, Emile Ford and the Checkmates, Jimmy Jones . . . All were stored in a cardboard shoebox and revered as if they were goblets of gold.

The record that thrilled me above all in 1960 didn't have the same effect on Linda – regrettably, as she naturally had a veto over our purchases. However, I had a stroke of luck one Saturday afternoon when Lily came home from lunchtime bingo in Shepherd's Bush having marked off a rare full house. She donated the cash I needed to buy the most exciting record I had heard to date: 'Shakin' All Over' by Johnny Kidd and the Pirates. As soon as the necessary 4s 6d (22½p in today's money) was in my hand I ran as fast as I could to get to Portobello Road before the record shop closed. I knew it was possible for me to cover the distance in ten minutes because that was my personal best for getting to Bevington School, which was about the same distance away.

Having equalled my personal best and acquired my prize, I returned triumphant to play it over and over again. The echo on the vocals, thumping bass and spine-tingling guitar solo were like nothing I'd ever heard before. It quite literally sent 'shivers down the backbone'. I was amazed to learn that Johnny Kidd and the Pirates were a British band (in fact Johnny Kidd hailed from Willesden, about three miles away, though in those days the world beyond the borders of North Kensington might as well not have existed for all I knew of it). Surely stuff this good only came from across the Atlantic?

My prejudice was evidently shared by the Americans, because while Johnny Kidd and the Pirates are still considered England's top rock 'n' roll band before the advent of the Beatles, despite being remembered for just this one song, their UK Number 1 wasn't a hit outside Europe. Many versions by other artists, however, were. Perhaps their evolving stage act, featuring full pirate costumes, was ahead of its time. Or maybe it was some of the dire material their record company made them commit to vinyl afterwards, unsure, in those early days, of how to capitalise on a rock 'n' roll hit. Whatever the case, the success of 'Shakin' All Over' was not to be repeated. The seminal influence of Johnny Kidd and the Pirates, though, lives on.

If I'd been aware, at ten years old, of the evolution of popular music, I might have appreciated the interesting detail that 'Shakin' All Over' was on HMV, the same label as 'Tap Your Feet', recorded 'With Vocal Refrain' thirty years earlier. Had I but realised it, I had at my fingertips the means to follow the trail from shellac to vinyl, from 78 to 45 and from Jack Hylton and His Orchestra to Johnny Kidd and the Pirates. Like a scientist observing a shift in the earth's formation, I was bearing witness to the birth of a new musical era while still having access to the one before last.

1961

Poetry in Motion

I SUPPOSE THAT, before the advent of the gramophone and the radio, when opportunities to listen to music were limited, most people had to make their own or hear none at all. I do not, of course, remember a time before those great inventions were commonplace, and neither would my parents' generation. But my father's pub piano-playing was a link to that earlier age before music and the means by which to hear it became part of the fabric of our daily lives.

One of my earliest memories is of Linda and me sitting atop the piano that Steve 'Ginger' Johnson was playing at a wedding reception somewhere in North Kensington. We were tiny, and a space had been cleared for us amid the accumulated pints donated to Steve by grateful guests who'd danced and sung to his repertoire of popular songs. 'Heart of My Hearts', 'On Mother Kelly's Doorstep', 'You Do Something to Me', 'Maybe It's Because I'm a Londoner', 'Apple Blossom Time' . . . Steve had enough material to fill a three-hour slot without repeats.

I don't know how my father became such a proficient pianist, but I do know that he played by ear, was unable to read a note of music and that he had the incredible gift of being able to reproduce any song he'd heard at the first attempt.

No doubt there were many other pianists who'd emerged untutored from working-class homes in the same way. However, supply never seemed to meet demand, which was why there were so many piano stools across London W10 and W11 upon which Steve was invited to park his posterior.

The songs our father played took root in our subconscious. As well as being present at lots of Steve's performances as toddlers, as we grew old enough to explore the streets around us we'd hear piano singsongs wafting out of pub doors tied open to let out the smoke. The loudest choruses, sung with the most fervour, could usually be heard just before closing time at around half-past two in the afternoon and eleven o'clock at night. On Sunday lunchtimes I sometimes joined other small children on the threshold of this forbidden territory to issue the plaintive cry: 'Dad! Mum says your dinner's ready!'

Running parallel with this irreligious musical education, we were absorbing a contrasting form of music through the hymns we sang at morning assembly. It seemed as if at least one teacher in every school could play the piano. Perhaps they were recruited specifically for that purpose. At Bevington it was the vivacious Miss Woofenden.

She it was who, early in 1961, asked her class of ten- and eleven-year-olds if anyone knew which record was Number 1 in the charts that week. This was during our music lesson, held in the main hall rather than the classroom, so that our teacher had access to the precious school piano.

I was the only child who put my hand up, blushing crimson

as I always did when I found myself the centre of attention, but confident of my answer: ' "Poetry in Motion" by Johnny Tillotson, Miss.'

Teen culture, born in the 1950s, had yet to trickle down to pre-teens as the decade ended and we still occupied a musical backwater compared with older, more sophisticated kids. Out in the wider world, consumers of pop music were beginning to give the home-grown variety a vote of confidence: 1961 was apparently the first-ever year in which the UK charts featured more artists from Britain than from the US. It was also the year Alan Freeman took over *Pick of the Pops* on the Light Programme, which was required listening on Sunday afternoons. So much so that at its peak, the show was being heard by practically a quarter of the population.

None of my friends, though, were interested in music. Tony Cox shared my passion for football, and I would sometimes see Dereck Tapper at Ladbroke Grove library, where I spent many happy hours indulging my other love, books. But Linda remained the only person with whom I could share my passion for music. Our record collection by now included 'Poetry in Motion' but not, alas, the recording made by Mr Tillotson. This was the worst of times for the Johnson household. Steve had stopped sending the weekly postal order for £6 10s decided upon by the courts (£1 10s for Lily and £2 10s each for Linda and me).

As our mother's heart condition worsened, and she spent more and more time in hospital and unable to work, we relied on Linda's increasingly wide portfolio of after-school jobs to finance our record-buying.

When we couldn't afford the 4s 6d for an original hit record, we'd go to Woolworth's and buy a cover version on the store's budget 'Embassy' label for a few shillings less. Our collection would eventually include covers of Bruce Channel's 'Hey! Baby', Roy Orbison's 'Running Scared' and Del Shannon's 'Runaway'.

The Embassy version was always released at the same time as the original, thus ensuring topicality. While I'm sure that the imitating performer must have been credited on the red Embassy label, I can't recall a single name, even though the records chalked up substantial sales.

Most of them, I later learned, were highly experienced session singers. They had to be good because there was no time for retakes – the breakneck schedules and tight budgets allowed for only half an hour per song. Though many did work under their professional names, pseudonyms were, not surprisingly, often used. So unbeknown to us, we probably possessed records made by some of the live singers we heard performing the current hits on the BBC.

In order to meet growing listener demand for more pop music, the Corporation was now forced to supplement its in-house orchestras, and bandleaders like Joe Loss and Billy Cotton, with musicians who could play pop hits live. While the big bandleaders still had a significant following among mums and dads, something more authentic was needed to appease the kids, a style that more closely resembled that of the pop groups to be imitated. So groups like Peter Jay and the Jaywalkers and Shane Fenton and the Fentones were being hired to play live on the Light Programme. Shane Fenton, whose real name was Bernard Jewry, would become better known in the 1970s and 1980s in another guise: Alvin Stardust.

By this time I did have one other means of slaking my thirst for pop songs by their original artists. One Christmas Lily had bought me a miniature crystal radio set with a string aerial, which unlocked the door to the three or four hours of music broadcast every night on Radio Luxembourg – accompanied by constant static.

As well as being pleased that I could answer Miss Woofenden's question in class that day I remember being surprised that she should ask it. She was getting on a bit – late twenties, I would say. While I was self-aware enough to realise that I was unusually young to be interested in pop music, I also knew that Miss Woofenden was unusually old. It was my first experience of perceiving that a teacher might be remotely interested in the things that interested Linda and me.

Perhaps Miss Woofenden was trying to broaden our horizons, but as far as I recall, this little incident was the only diversion at Bevington from our usual diet of hymns. While never inspired by the religion that underpinned them, I loved belting out the songs. At morning assembly I would join in the cheery rendition of ditties such as 'All Things Bright and Beautiful' with gusto.

At Sloane Grammar School, to which I moved on later that year after passing my Eleven-Plus, the hymns reflected a more muscular Christianity and the girls, who had been the most enthusiastic singers at Bevington, were no longer present. This was an all-boys school.

'Onward Christian Soldiers' was one of the Sloane favourites. It had a masculine appeal that brought out the best in us boys, even the ones who mumbled through assembly hymns, moving their lips just enough to satisfy the scrutiny of the teachers watching from the stage for any signs of insubordination.

Other songs improved our vocabularies. Singing them was like being given an English lesson. When we first opened our hymnbooks to embark on 'He Who Would Valiant Be', John Bunyan's words towered before us like a rock face waiting to be climbed. A deep breath and off we went:

> He who would valiant be 'gainst all disaster,
> Let him in constancy follow the Master.
> There's no discouragement shall make him once relent
> His first avowed intent to be a pilgrim.

How I loved those words that my mouth had never uttered and my ears had never heard: 'valiant', 'constancy', 'discouragement', 'relent', 'intent' and, later in the hymn, 'confound' and 'dismal'. Most of all I loved the strange, mellifluous 'pilgrim'.

After a while the hymnbooks became redundant as we only ever sang the same five or six hymns in rotation and soon committed their words to memory through constant repetition.

'Jerusalem' was my first experience of proper poetry, Blake's lyric swelling my chest with an emotion I didn't fully understand: a sort of puzzled pride. This wasn't the same kind of music as 'Poetry in Motion', but it was poetic, and it certainly moved me.

1962

Sealed with a Kiss

I'VE LEARNED THAT the world came close to nuclear annihilation in 1962 but I don't remember anything about the Cuban missile crisis. I was blissfully unaware of any sense of impending doom, which I suppose is the best state to be in when doom decides to impend.

A little over a week before the crisis began, on 5 October 1962, the Beatles released their first single. I was largely unaware of that as well, which marks out 1962 as the last year in which the Beatles weren't an integral part of my life.

I do recall seeing a photo of this obscure Liverpudlian group, at the time 'Love Me Do' was released, in a weekly pop magazine to which Linda subscribed. Even our mother, as a born-and-bred Scouser, took a mild interest. Ringo was still sporting an Elvis Presley quiff and a streak of grey hair that seems subsequently to have been dyed out of existence.

The relationship between Linda and me was undergoing an evolutionary change. She was becoming less like a sister and more like a mother as Lily spent more and more time in hospital, leaving her daughter to take command of grappling with the debts created by our mother's incapacity and our father's indolence. The age difference between us – two years and eight months – was also suddenly opening a wider social chasm. She was fifteen and would be leaving school the following spring, while I was still in my first full year at Sloane. Her friends seemed more like adults; mine were still children. She was acquiring boyfriends; my voice had yet to break.

I was very unhappy at my new school. The contrast with Bevington was stark and isolating – only two other boys had transferred to Sloane from my primary school, and one of them was in a different class. The journey there and back was daunting enough: a quarter of a mile's walk to Latimer Road tube station, my books stuffed into a duffel bag slung across my shoulder, four stops on the Metropolitan Line to Hammersmith, through the arcade and across to the bus stop opposite the Hammersmith Palais to catch the number 11, which took half an hour to snake through Hammersmith, Fulham and Chelsea to the bus stop near Lots Road power station.

When I finally reached school, there was a further challenge to be overcome. At each gate stood a sixth-form prefect waiting to report any boy who arrived a second later than nine o'clock. Persistent lateness could (and did in my case) lead to a caning, delivered with relish by our headmaster, the stick-thin, sharp-featured Dr Henry.

I hated most of my lessons. Particularly Latin, in which I barely got past *amo, amas, amat*, and French with Mr Harris (nicknamed 'Dolly' for reasons I never discovered), who was possibly the most boring teacher in the world – though I can't in all fairness blame dear old Dolly for my complete lack of competence in the subject.

I even dreaded games and PE because of having to get undressed in front of the other boys. Every one of them seemed to be wearing brilliant white vests and pants, so immaculate they appeared to have been newly purchased for each PE period, and their socks had holes only where their feet went in. I'd never worn a vest in my life and it's best not to dwell on the state of my underpants. As for my socks, let's just say they were well ventilated. Lily received financial help to buy my uniform (complete with a superfluous cap and a dark blue raincoat belted at the waist), but she had to find the money for everything worn underneath and that meant a certain amount of make do and mend.

And there was the dreaded dinner-money ritual, presided over by my form teacher, Mr Woosnam, every Monday morning. He would call out our names in alphabetical order, whereupon the bidden child had to approach his desk at the front of the class and hand over his dinner money for the week ahead. When my name was called I was forced to shout out, 'Free, sir.' Mr Woosnam meant no harm and was, I'm sure, completely unaware of the anguish this caused the only 'free' kid in the class. Even if there had been more of us the effect would have been equally humiliating.

The saving grace was a music teacher at Sloane who was a worthy successor to Miss Woofenden. Mr Dearlove was an urbane character in his late thirties, with thick, wavy, elaborately styled hair, a strand of which always fell across his forehead, like a stray leaf hanging down from a flower display.

giving him an absentminded air. He had a cheery disposition and a fondness for three-piece suits.

Mr Dearlove auditioned all the new boys for the school choir during our first few weeks at Sloane. His principal aim seemed to be to identify some sopranos who could compensate musically for the absence of any female voices. No doubt our counterparts in their first year at Carlyle Grammar School for Girls, who congregated in the next building, along Hortensia Road, behind a high and forbidding brick wall, were being simultaneously auditioned for baritones.

Having impressed Mr Dearlove with my singing ability and the purity of my unbroken voice, I found myself committed to spending my lunch breaks practising for the 1961 Christmas concert. But Mr Dearlove's lunchtime choir practice became the highlight of my school day. We had two pieces to master for the concert. One was a piece of sacred music by Claudio Monteverdi, which we had to sing in the original Italian. I can't recall the name of the piece, which is a pity, since to this day it's the only Italian I've ever spoken.

The other was 'Habanera' from Bizet's *Carmen*, perhaps his most famous aria apart from the Toreador song. This one was to be sung in English:

Love will like a wild birdling fly, careering whither it may please,
Vainly to him for help we cry, but 'tis his fancy to displease.

Mr Dearlove rehearsed us well and gave me a glorious introduction to opera but, in the end, I let him down by failing to turn up for the concert.

At the beginning of December I made a meal of an eye injury

sustained in the school gym to such an extent that I convinced both my mother and our GP to keep me off school until April the following year.

So I began 1962 educating myself at leisure at home. Throughout our childhood Lily had ensured that we had comics to read as well as library books to borrow. By now Linda's *Bunty* and my *Hotspur* had given way to *Billy Fury Magazine* and *Charles Buchan's Football Monthly* respectively. But I had kept all my back copies of *Hotspur* and during this glorious spell of educational inactivity I read them all again. It was around this time that my mother increased the paper bill at the newsagent's opposite our house in Walmer Road by ordering a new magazine, the title of which demonstrated its worthy purpose.

Knowledge was a collection of thick, beautifully illustrated pages that could be bound between laminated covers by means of a set of thin metal rods. Lily shelled out an extra half-crown for the binding kit. She had never been able to acquire an encyclopaedia, so I suppose she saw this as the next best thing. I learned a lot about the Phoenicians, Roman Britain and Hereward the Wake from reading *Knowledge* and had even begun to bind the editions into Volume 1 before Linda was forced to cancel the order because we couldn't afford it.

By now she had a steady boyfriend, a local jack-the-lad by the name of Jimmy Carter. My sister had matured early, already having gone on several one-off dates, including an outing with an Italian student who'd chatted her up on the tube between Hammersmith and Latimer Road. If they'd stayed together, he could have helped me with the Monteverdi.

With Jimmy it was serious. He was to be a fixture in our lives for at least a year, even becoming engaged to be married to my industrious sister.

I liked Jimmy and, more importantly, so did Lily. However, I don't think she ever saw him as son-in-law material and Linda may well have felt the same. Round our way, an engagement was rarely the precursor of a wedding. Couples got engaged without the slightest intention of getting married. Jimmy was a man of considerable charm and, in addition to an affection for Linda, the three of us – Lily, Jimmy and I – shared a penchant for cigarettes.

My sister never smoked. She was too sensible for that. But I took up the habit at the age of twelve. My strict(ish) mother was surprisingly indulgent, sometimes even slipping me a packet of ten Rothman's King Size, a perk of one of her latest part-time jobs in a tobacconist's kiosk next to Ladbroke Grove station. They were our little secret, passed to me surreptitiously to avoid my sister's stern disapproval.

I would smoke on the way to school, permitted then on the top deck of the bus (as well as on the tube, and more or less everywhere else). Although Linda and I took the same route in the mornings, we never travelled together. She had to be in earlier than I did and liked to go with her older and more sophisticated friends. Even so, I never lit a fag until I had passed the bus stop where they all got off – Fulham Cross, a couple of miles before mine – in case one of her friends saw me.

Having finally returned to school that April, I didn't have to endure it for too long before the summer holidays and the greatest adventure of my life to date: my first trip abroad. I had never been out of the country and it would be another twenty years before I left these shores again.

I was bound for Denmark with a large contingent of London's waifs and strays, courtesy of the Children's Country Holiday Fund (CCHF), a charity founded in Dickensian times to give slum children a chance to experience the fresh air of the countryside. If this sounds like a stroke of luck, that's what it was: usually these holidays were in England but I had the good fortune to be selected in one of only a couple of years when they were offered further afield, thanks to the generosity of the London *Evening Standard* newspaper, which enabled CCHF to fund the use of a Danish horticultural college near Esbjerg while the local students were on their own summer break. Linda had been on one three years earlier – to Guildford. So whereas Linda got Surrey, I got Scandinavia.

I had a glorious fortnight in Denmark, much of it spent showing off to the girl who had become the focus of my youthful adoration. For among my new experiences in this exotic land of blue skies and wide, open spaces was a tender east-meets-west romance (Edna was from Whitechapel).

After the first week we were taking long walks together in the peaceful, verdant Danish countryside, during which poor Edna was subjected to my singing as I displayed my profound knowledge of contemporary song lyrics, gleaned from another purchase from the newsagent's in Walmer Road. *Record Song Book* provided the words to chart records ('B' sides as well as 'A' sides), printed on paper so cheap you could still see the wood pulp. It was published every month for 3d.

Edna was thus treated to exclusive, word-perfect renditions of 'Things', 'A Picture of You' and 'I Remember You', Top 20 hits that August for Bobby Darin, Joe Brown and Frank Ifield respectively, as we wandered unaccompanied through country lanes. In a pre-pubescent golden haze of innocence we kissed – just the once – and Edna told me that she loved me.

We vowed to meet again but never did. After we returned home I wrote to her at the address she'd given me in Whitechapel Road, where she lived with her mother and four siblings. She made no mention of a father. There was no reply. She probably dreaded me singing to her again.

When I arrived back in London on the train from Harwich it was Linda who met me. Lily had gone into hospital for yet more tests and treatment. At home Linda produced two records she'd bought while I was away, 'She's Not You' by Elvis and 'Sealed with a Kiss' by Brian Hyland, which I'd heard on the radio and hankered after before my trip to Denmark.

'She's Not You' was a return to form by Presley following some dreary singles released on the back of his turgid films but Hyland's plaintive ballad now held a new and special significance for me. Its haunting harmonica introduction and resonant lyrics about saying goodbye for the summer invoked in me a delicious sadness as I thought of Edna and the single kiss we'd shared.

1963

All My Loving

Sexual intercourse began
In nineteen sixty-three
(which was rather late for me) –
Between the end of the Chatterley ban
And the Beatles' first LP.

IF IT WAS rather late for Philip Larkin it was a bit too early for me, but the chaste kiss that sealed my romance with Edna the previous year was by far the most thrilling thing I'd ever done with another human being.

As I carried that sweet memory into 1963, I was certainly more interested in girls than I had been previously but all the innuendoes and insinuations of the sex-saturated Profumo scandal still went completely over my head. I didn't understand what was meant by 'living off immoral earnings' and couldn't make sense of the complex chain of events linking Stephen Ward with Captain Yevgeny Ivanov, John Profumo, Christine Keeler and Mandy Rice-Davies. Perhaps I wasn't alone in that respect.

My mother certainly wasn't going to be the one to explain it all to me. While she devoured the latest news in the *Daily Sketch* during her brief morning break, sitting with her feet up, drinking tea and smoking one of her razor-halved cigarettes, she avoided any discussion with me that might remotely touch upon the birds and the bees.

It had been left to my sister to relate the basic facts of life, which she had done in a difficult conversation one evening when Lily was safely out of the way. Now Linda displayed the smug superiority that came naturally to a fifteen-year-old girl with a steady boyfriend in the presence of an immature younger brother. She pretended to understand every aspect of the scandal and told me patronisingly that I couldn't because I was too young.

It was impossible for me to confide in her or my mother about the way I was feeling; about the maelstrom of emotions raging through me like an electric current. I think I fancied Mandy Rice-Davies, considering her the prettiest of the two girls at the centre of the Profumo storm, whose pictures were everywhere. If 'fancying' meant nothing more carnal than taking delight in gazing on a woman's countenance, that's about where I was with Mandy.

There were other women. While in hospital having my appendix removed at the beginning of 1963, as that historically terrible winter tightened its grip on the country, I fell in love with a French nurse who came to tuck me in every night. And Linda's red-headed, freckled friend Kathleen Kelly made me feel as if my insides were dissolving whenever she deigned to acknowledge my existence upon her very occasional visits to our house.

Finding myself attracted to these older women may have had

something to do with the fact that I hardly ever encountered any girls of my own age. Edna had been a rare exception in unusual circumstances. As a pupil at an all-boys school, I'd had to go to Denmark to meet a female contemporary from London.

While there was a distinct sense of community in Walmer Road, with the newsagent's opposite and a corner shop at the end of the terrace, I had no close friendships there with any boys, let alone girls, the same age as me. Gerald Wright, who'd lived further down Walmer Road, close to the junction with Bramley Road, had been my only local mate before his family was allocated a council house in Basingstoke and moved out of London. Tony Cox, my bosom buddy at primary school, was not far away in Lancaster Road, but we had grown apart even before we both went to Sloane as two thirds of the trio from Bevington. While his wonderful mother Pat had become a firm friend of Lily's as a result of our childhood alliance, Tony and I now had little to do with one another.

Dereck Tapper, the other Bevington boy who moved on to Sloane, lived on the other side of the Portobello Road, much too far away to be 'local'. He was also immersed in a studious phase and wanted no distractions.

At school I had teamed up with two separate groups, one from Shepherd's Bush and one from Fulham. Foremost among the Shepherd's Bush set was my fellow aspiring musician Andrew Wiltshire, slightly built, dark and uproariously funny. Just as I was teaching myself to play the guitar, he was learning the drums.

Andrew lived close to Wormwood Scrubs, a fifteen-minute walk away from me down Latimer Road. He had been introduced to jazz, soul and R&B by his two older brothers, one of whom was a Mod, a style and culture we admired. Andrew had a liking for Georgie Fame, Geno Washington and the Ram Jam Band, and American artists such as Marvin Gaye.

I was also friends with his mate John Williams, who lived on the Wormholt estate in Acton. The three of us loved the Goons, thought we were 'cool' and postured accordingly for the big Sloane school photo, the kind taken with a single camera rolling across a long line of schoolboys, arranged in several rows, which afforded a mischievous pupil the chance to get himself in twice if he was fast enough.

One of Andrew's claims to fame was that he'd had a genuine brush with pop stardom. That winter, with snow lying thick everywhere, he had got involved in a play snowball fight with some children in the front garden of one of the exclusive houses in Roehampton we used to pass every week on our way to and from Sloane's sports ground.

Andrew was alone when he responded to the snowball attack. He and the small children who'd ambushed him were having great fun when a parent came to the door of the grand house. He invited Andrew in for a hot drink and some cake. The father of these children turned out to be none other than Pat Boone, the American singer who'd been the second biggest-selling recording artist of the late 1950s behind Elvis Presley.

There followed several weekends of Andrew being picked up from home in a chauffeur-driven car and conveyed to Roehampton to play with the junior Boones. In fact, this went on right up to the time when the children's father finished his UK tour, gave up the rented house and took the family back to the US.

The big music venue round our way was the Hammersmith Palais, which had begun to offer a reduced entry fee to teenagers on Monday evenings for what would in the future become known as a 'disco', although that term did not exist in London in 1963. Anyway, it was a dance where records were played, young people could show off their prowess at the latest dance crazes and partners were not necessarily required.

This was an innovation for the Palais, where Joe Loss was the resident bandleader and ballroom dancing the preferred pursuit of its regular clientele. It was probably something that was happening everywhere as the waltz gave way to the Twist, and sequinned gowns to mini-skirts. The two forms of dancing were at first the preserve of different generations – until older people started doing the Twist, forcing the young to abandon Chubby Checker for the next new dance craze unsullied by parental approval.

Linda and her fiancé, Jimmy Carter, were regulars at the Palais on Monday evenings and I longed to go as well, but it was for over-eighteens only. Strictly speaking Linda and Jimmy would have been equally disbarred by the age limit, but they were old enough to pass for eighteen. Not that there was any necessity to provide proof of identity: a bouncer on the door simply looked each entrant up and down as they wandered in. But I felt I was far too fresh-faced to pass even this cursory check.

Andrew's Mod brother used to go to the Palais a lot and he assured us that if we arrived early enough, before the bouncer began his evening's work in earnest, with somebody older (like him), we would be able to sidestep this crude appraisal. One Monday evening we tried our luck, succeeded and thereafter became regular attendees, much to Linda's chagrin. This was her stamping ground, upon which I was not supposed to intrude. I was not keen, either, on being chaperoned, though I knew she would be watching out for me all the same. So inside the dance hall we kept our distance from each other, which wasn't difficult in that vast hangar of a space.

For the older teens this was boy-meets-girl territory. There was a protocol to be followed. The evening would begin with the girls dancing round their handbags while the blokes congregated at the bars. As the night wore on some liaisons were formed without significantly depleting the handbag dancers until, near the end, the lights went down and the slow records came on. That was when the boys moved in for a smooch. The unapproached girls were left to guard the bags.

Steady couples such as Linda and Jimmy were in a different category. They generally mixed with other couples, sitting round tables in the bar area looking adult and taking to the floor only occasionally.

A third species, at the other end of the age scale from us, were the 'Palais Prowlers', sleazy older men who came alone and patrolled the dark edges of the auditorium looking for single women.

Andrew and I watched all this dispassionately. We knew the girls wouldn't dance with us even if they were our age. There seemed to be some kind of rule that girls were only interested in older boys. In any case I was far too shy to ask for a dance.

Nor were we interested in alcohol. The real excitement for me was listening to my favourite records being played at an impressive volume for hours on end. It was at the Palais that I first heard the debut single by a new group called the Rolling Stones, became aware of Little Stevie Wonder, an American singer only my age, thrilled to the Searchers' 'Sweets for My Sweet' and 'Do You Love Me?' by Brian Poole and the Tremeloes. On the dance floor the girls did the Locomotion, the Watusi and the Pony. If the 'swinging sixties' were happening anywhere, they were happening at the Hammersmith Palais on Monday evenings in 1963.

As the year progressed I began to spend more time with my Fulham friends. The clincher was this: while Andrew's house was nearer (and his parents always welcoming), all we could really do there was mess around in the room he shared with his Mod brother. On the other hand, the central figure of the Fulham set, Colin James, had his own basement retreat, down a flight of stairs beyond the prying eyes of his parents and four younger siblings.

I was always closer to Andrew, geographically and emotionally, but I wanted to be mates with both groups. Although Andrew and Colin were in the same class at school, they were never friends with each other, which ruled out going around together. So I bounced back and forth between the two.

Colin was a scion of a prosperous, middle-class family who lived in a four-storey house near Parsons Green. He seemed to be in permanent rebellion against his background, to the despair of his lovely parents. He picked fights with his father and longed to be rated as the toughest kid in the school. He adored the Rolling Stones, whose demeanour of youthful revolt he copied, and the James Bond novels of Ian Fleming.

What was more, whereas the only girl at Andrew's was his little sister, Colin had two female friends of our own age, Pauline Bright and Yvonne Stacey, pupils at Carlyle, who lived near him and often came round to hang out in his sanctuary. So it isn't difficult to see the attractions Fulham had to offer.

The downside was that visiting Colin involved the same

journey as I took to school and meant travelling back late at night. But there were no curbs on my freedom. I wasn't subjected to the same parental control as my sister had been at the same age. Our mother seemed less fretful about my whereabouts. Perhaps she made the not unreasonable assumption that boys were in less danger out on the streets than girls. The streets of North Kensington, however, always seemed dangerous enough to me.

Walking home from Latimer Road station to Walmer Road in the dark, I carried a steel comb in my hand and would keep as far away from the houses as possible in case I was jumped. I'd been attacked a couple of years before by a gang in Oldham Street, which was on my way home from the tube station, only just managing to outrun my pursuers and their shouted warning never to set foot in their street again. The year before that a man had held me hostage in the middle of Ladbroke Grove, threatening to cut me with a piece of broken glass held close to my left eye. I forget what he was demanding, but what he needed was medical attention. And what I needed, I'd decided then, was to be more careful.

Violence was a part of growing up in North Kensington. Whether it was the domestic violence that had been inflicted on my mother and so many other women, the horrific killings at 10 Rillington Place a few streets away, for which John Christie had been hanged a decade earlier, the race riots, the terrible murder of Kelso Cochrane or, on a more mundane level, the daily beatings meted out by our teachers at Bevington Primary School (a cane across the hand for the boys and a ruler applied to the legs of the girls).

There were also the daily confrontations in the playground

or on the streets that all boys had to endure. I could fight a bit and run pretty fast, but I agreed with Baden-Powell about the importance of being prepared. Hence the steel comb.

I was beginning to carry a bit of money, too, having acquired two jobs with Jimmy Carter's older brother John, helping him on his milk round all day on a Saturday and on Sunday mornings and on his paraffin round two evenings a week. Unlike Linda, who'd had to use her earnings to pay off Lily's debts, I was free to spend my money as I pleased. Apart from the odd request for a shilling for the gas meter, neither my sister nor my mother troubled me for a contribution.

As a result I was gradually building my own record collection, a separate entity from the one Linda and I had put together over the past three years; a collection that would be an uncompromising reflection of my taste.

With much of the early repertoire of the Beatles and the Rolling Stones consisting of the American R&B artists who had influenced them growing up, there was an upsurge of interest in the music of Chuck Berry, Bo Diddley, Muddy Waters, Sonny Boy Williamson et al. They recorded on the Chess label in the US, but their records were largely unavailable in the UK until the Pye record company responded to public demand and began to release them on a 'Pye International' label.

Even then, not all record shops stocked them, but in a little place near our sports ground in Roehampton I struck gold, finding Chuck's *School Days* EP (extended play record), which also featured 'Johnny B. Goode' and 'Sweet Little Sixteen'. A significant Pye International collection was soon in place.

I had been a Beatles devotee since hearing their second single, 'Please Please Me', on the hospital radio after having my appendix removed the previous year. While Linda had taken an interest in 'Love Me Do', it had never ignited a real passion in her for the Fab Four and hadn't been added to our joint treasure trove of singles. Lily took pride in the new status the band were bringing to her native city but that didn't extend to a liking for their music, or indeed that of any of the other groups that emerged in their wake from Liverpool.

I hadn't bought the early Beatles records because I wanted to save my precious earnings for music that few other people had. I could listen to Beatles records at Colin James's house, because he had them all. Indeed, it was Colin's collection that inspired my first bid for pop stardom. Along with Jimmy Robb, another schoolfriend, Colin and I formed our own band, the Vampires, with occasional input from a big blond boy originally from the Channel Islands called Lilliput. We would play in Colin's Fulham basement, imagining ourselves in the Cavern Club in Liverpool.

So it wasn't the Beatles first LP, immortalised in that Larkin poem, that sealed my bond with John, Paul, George and Ringo; it was the second, released at the end of 1963. *With the Beatles* was the first LP I ever bought and it cost half what I'd earned from a weekend on the milk float and two freezing evenings delivering paraffin.

I purchased it at the record shop in the Hammersmith station arcade and made a point of taking it out of the plastic bag in which it was handed to me so that the cover image of the Fab Four, dressed in black polo-neck jumpers and gazing out from half-shadow, was visible to my fellow travellers on the tube to Latimer Road. Those four young men had revolutionised British popular culture during 1963 and would go on to conquer the world.

That evening I sat alone in our 'parlour' to listen to my new record. Lily was lying in hospital and Linda was out somewhere. It was just a week or so after the awful night late in 1963 when my mother, who had resisted the operation she so desperately needed, became so ill that she had to be rushed to hospital in the small hours. It would, Linda told me, be an extended stay.

It was exceptionally cold so I turned on both bars of our electric heater, which presented the unconvincing façade of a real fire created by a red bulb at the back. Its scarlet light was the only illumination as I sat in the fake leather armchair, transfixed by the music, getting up only to turn the record over from side one to side two and back again, over and over again for hours. From 'It Won't Be Long' to 'Money', all fourteen tracks seemed to me to be the greatest music ever made, with 'All My Loving' the highlight. Any other recording artist with a song like that would have released it as a single rather than 'waste' it on an LP. It was a harbinger of what was to come.

That year I entered my teens and on that night in November the Beatles entered my soul. I would be With the Beatles for the rest of my life.

1964

You Really Got Me

MY MOTHER DIED on 4 March 1964. Her final stay in hospital lasted five months, culminating in the surgery she dreaded, which led to the outcome she had feared: death, at just forty-two, the age at which both her mother and grandmother had died. Just as I was experiencing the hormonal explosion that made my blood run richer and my heart beat faster, that seemed to open all life's possibilities, Lily's life ended.

It had been an unrelentingly hard one. Denied educational opportunities throughout a tough Liverpool childhood and plagued by illness, at eighteen she grasped the chance to escape a tyrannical father by joining the NAAFI in London upon the outbreak of war. After walking out with several soldier admirers, she was swept off her feet by the dashing Lance Corporal Steve Johnson, who played the piano at army concerts in immaculate white gloves. He took his new wife back to his home territory in North Kensington to occupy the awful slums into which my sister and I had been born. Lily deserved better than a philandering husband, a debilitating heart condition and an early death.

Linda had always believed this better life would materialise after Lily had undergone a ground-breaking operation to replace the mitral valve in her heart. We'd soon be allocated the council house that was long overdue, she reasoned. Hammersmith Hospital would repair Lily's heart, London County Council would rescue us from the slums and Lily would have what she'd always dreamed of: her own front door.

Linda had bought our mother the latest Bachelors LP for Christmas (amid the explosion of British music talent, they remained the only group Lily liked). After she had finished opening her presents on Christmas Day 1963, her hospital bed still strewn with wrapping paper, she handed us the record to take back with us to Walmer Road for safekeeping, so that she could listen to it when she got home. That evening we had carefully placed it in our record collection, alongside *With the Beatles*, to await her return.

But Lily never came back and the record went unplayed. Two of the tracks, 'Diane' and 'I Believe', were released as singles and, as if in tribute, dominated the Top 10 the week she died. The album remained in our collection, a forlorn reminder of when our mother had shape and form, likes and dislikes, views and opinions, before she became just a memory.

~

I'm not sure how I ended up owning Bert Weedon's *Play in a Day*. It probably came with the Spanish guitar my mother bought for me out of her pools win.

I now know how influential Bert's self-help manual has been to all kinds of musicians, with great guitarists such as Eric

Clapton, George Harrison and Keith Richards having paid homage to its instructive powers. I doubt, though, that anybody actually learned to play in a single day – a year, perhaps, or a decade. All I can say is that I sat in my squalid bedroom, with its damp, peeling wallpaper hidden behind the centrefold photographs of football teams torn from *Charles Buchan's Football Monthly*, perched on the edge of my bed, strumming away remorselessly for month after month without making much progress.

I recall that Bert's book had 'Drink to Me Only with Thine Eyes' or some such song scored for those who wanted to pick out a tune, but all I wanted to do was strum, like Lonnie. I was interested in chord formations rather than melodies, in rhythm rather than lead guitar. I was far from being a natural but by 1964 it all seemed to be falling into place. By then I knew my chords, I could strum rhythmically – I could even knock out the occasional folk song, putting down the plectrum to 'pick' rather than 'pluck'.

My expanding Pye International collection was providing me with plenty of source material. I'd purchased every Chuck Berry single, EP and LP on the label, which wasn't that many. Such was my appetite for his music that I wrote to London Records to find out if there was any chance of accessing the material by the great man I'd heard had been released in Germany. I received a typed reply informing me that their Chuck Berry catalogue had been 'deleted'.

Jimmy Carter had also been 'deleted' from my sister's life after she found out that her fiancé was heading to the West End for extracurricular activities, having kissed her goodnight outside our front door. Linda was now 'going steady' with Mike Whitaker, who was at least five years older than her and drove his own car. Mike's quiet sophistication and diverse taste in music enhanced my education. He'd brought to our Dansette in the 'parlour' of 6 Walmer Road albums by an obscure young American folk singer named Bob Dylan, the Belgian *chansons* of Jacques Brel and the coolest record of the moment, 'Green Onions' by Booker T. and the MGs.

Our television, while it opened up new horizons to us in general, was not exactly a rich seam of pop music until the advent in 1963 of *Ready, Steady, Go!*, the innovative Friday night ITV show that provided a platform for both new artists and the big names to play their latest singles and pioneered interaction with studio audiences.

There were only two channels – the BBC and ITV ('the other side') – and back then, if you wanted to watch a particular programme, you had to make sure you were at home to see it at the time the broadcaster chose to air it. *Ready, Steady, Go!* had the perfect slot, which it made the most of by opening every programme with its trademark slogan 'The weekend starts here!'

The BBC, always more reactive than proactive, offered shows like *Juke Box Jury*, hosted by David Jacobs, where celebrity panellists predicted which new records would be 'hits' and which 'misses'. Their first stab at a pop programme, *Six-Five Special*, had been screened in the late 1950s, produced by Jack Good. It was very popular, but when the BBC meddled with Good's non-stop music format he defected to ITV, where he would be free of the influence of the BBC's public-service remit, and created *Oh Boy!*. The ITV show overwhelmed *Six-Five Special* in the ratings and helped to launch the career of Cliff Richard, who appeared on it regularly. Both of these pioneering programmes had come and gone before we had a television, and I don't remember seeing either of them.

Eventually the BBC were persuaded that what teenage pop fans wanted was live performers and uninterrupted music rather than family-oriented musical parlour games or artists appearing in one-off guest spots on Saturday night variety shows. In 1964 they launched *Top of the Pops*, initially from a studio housed in a former church hall in Manchester. Although it could never have been described as innovative – being a chart-based show, it featured acts and singles that were already selling – it did help to push records up the charts, and it gave us the current hits and the bands in the flesh (even if they were miming). *Top of the Pops* would continue for forty-two years and become a national institution. It was the only TV programme I rarely missed.

Also in 1964 came the pirate radio stations, spearheaded by Radio Caroline, which was soon joined by others, including Radio London. The pirates were able to circumvent the UK ban on commercial radio, the BBC monopoly and all of the regulations, including the 'needle time' agreement, by broadcasting from ships anchored in international waters, just outside the three-mile offshore limit of British sovereignty. Unhindered by the restrictions of legislation, they played pop records round the clock, sometimes airing new singles before they were even officially released. At the time I didn't have a radio capable of picking up these stations, so I was still denied proper access to the music I craved.

For my fourteenth birthday in May, Mike and Linda bought me a present so wonderful it might have come from a celestial source: tickets to see Chuck Berry at the Hammersmith Odeon.

Just as I'd been made aware of Chuck through the British bands that had recorded his songs, so had millions of others. Now he was the headline act on a rock 'n' roll tour of the country, supported by a rockabilly legend, Carl Perkins, of 'Blue Suede Shoes' fame, and a couple of new British groups promoting their debut singles.

There were three tickets, for Linda, Mike and me, but when Mike had to drop out at the last minute because of a work commitment, Linda suggested giving the spare ticket to her schoolfriend, the aforementioned Kathleen Kelly. Completely unaware of my secret infatuation with Kathleen, she even asked if I would mind. I managed to sound casual as I gave my consent. Alas, I was immature even compared with girls my own age. Kathleen was a contemporary of my sister's and way out of my league. Still, I was entitled to dream.

Having been presented with the perfect opportunity to press my suit with Kathleen, I wished I was more like my happy-go-lucky friend Andrew Wiltshire. He was a 'doer', uninhibited by shyness, whereas I was burdened by timidity and lacked Linda's adamantine nature. I fantasised that I was taking a gorgeous redhead to a rock concert for which my sister also happened to have a ticket and set off that evening with hope in my heart.

Unfortunately, as we took our seats high in the upper tier, Linda plonked herself between her friend and me. My disappointment, though crushing, was brief: once the concert began, such earthly considerations hardly seemed to matter.

First there was a spirited rendition of 'Tobacco Road' by the

Nashville Teens, of whom nobody had ever heard before. In fact they came from Weybridge rather than Nashville, but that song was a hit for them in the States as well as in Britain. Next up were the Animals, performing their debut single (and minor hit), a rock treatment of 'Baby Let Me Take You Home' – an old US folk song I knew as 'Baby Let Me Follow You Down', from the Bob Dylan album to which Mike had introduced me.

Then the lights were lowered and the Animals launched into the climax of their set, another revamped track from that same Dylan album. 'The House of the Rising Sun' would be a massive hit around the world, but I doubt its effect would ever have been as profound as it was when it was first played to the audiences on that tour. It is said that it was the response of these live crowds that led to the Animals' decision to nip into a little studio off Kingsway in London between tour dates and record it as a single. Today it is credited by some as the first folk-rock hit. With its slow build-up, dark lyrics, Eric Burdon's powerful vocal and, above all, that incredible organ solo by Alan Price, lit by a single spotlight on the Odeon stage, it was an absolute showstopper. Except that the show was just getting going.

Still to come was the headline act, Chuck Berry, with his big white Gibson guitar, doing his famous duck walk backwards and forwards across the stage. I knew every word of every song: 'Maybellene', 'School Day', 'Memphis, Tennessee', 'Roll Over Beethoven' . . . all rock 'n' roll mini-operas performed with wit and verve.

I glanced sideways occasionally to catch Kathleen's perfect profile and to try to ascertain if she was impressed by my musical hero. I think she was. This, however, was no place for conversation. But outside the Odeon afterwards she went straight off to catch her bus home to Fulham and I never saw her again. Still, we had shared a magical evening: me, Chuck and Kathleen Kelly.

～

My solitary autodidactic efforts in my bedroom with Bert Weedon and my guitar may not have made me fully proficient, but I was without doubt the finest guitarist in Colin James's basement. None of the other Vampires could play a note, and with Jimmy Robb's drumkit composed of Tupperware bowls (Lonnie would have been proud of us), our sessions were an exercise in imagination and improvisation rather than musicianship.

The captive audience of Yvonne Stacey and Pauline Bright displayed a healthy indifference to our artistry. If they ever screamed, as young girls were inclined to do at Beatles concerts, it was likely to have been from pain as we massacred another of their favourite songs.

With Yvonne and Pauline, I learned that platonic friendship across the gender divide was possible. Colin had grown up with them, so he knew that already. But there was nothing platonic about the friendship we struck up with two other girls who entered our social circle early that year. Christine Roberts and Susan Kelly weren't Carlyle Grammar School girls. Christine, who went to a secondary modern in Parsons Green, lived in a block of flats on the Hurlingham estate with her parents and younger sister. She was Colin's girlfriend.

Susan Kelly (no relation to Kathleen) was mine. She lived at the Fulham end of the King's Road in a house we never entered but towards which my gaze is still drawn on the odd occasion I drive by it. She was a bit of a mystery, was Susan. I don't know which school she attended, only that it wasn't Carlyle. She claimed to be at stage school and to have been a finalist in a TV talent contest, but I was never sure if that was true.

Colin had met Christine at a party and was soon 'going out' with her. He suggested that she bring a friend so that we could make up a foursome. The friend was Susan. So it was a kind of blind date. We all met up at Christine's house one Saturday morning and decided we'd go to Carnaby Street. Colin and I had been there once, but talked as if we were there all the time. Within a couple of hours, as we were looking in the window of a chic West End clothes shop, Susan reached for my hand.

I knew that we'd properly assumed the status of 'boyfriend' and 'girlfriend' when I was invited to accompany her to her cousin's wedding a few weeks after my mother died. I wore my very best clothes, a pale blue collarless Beatles jacket with tight black trousers, a 'long john' white shirt and Chelsea boots.

It was the first occasion I remember drinking alcohol, but it wasn't the small quantity of beer that heightened my emotions: it was the perfumed thrill of being close to the voluptuous Susan at a gathering of elders where we were treated as young adults rather than kids. Halfway through the evening the DJ announced that he had a copy of the newly released Beatles single 'Can't Buy Me Love'. It turned a good evening into a perfect one.

Susan had the short bobbed haircut I liked and was very attractive. I remember one of her relatives saying we made a lovely couple, and that night, we did. However, the truth was that I always hankered after Colin's girlfriend. I even fantasised about becoming a soldier and going away, returning years later to sweep my secret love off her feet (Colin having, with luck, conveniently deserted Christine by then). Don't ask me why the soldier bit was in there. I spent my infant years dreading being called up for National Service and, after its abolition, the rest of my childhood fearing another world war in which I'd be expected to fight. Perhaps my imagination was caught by the classic recruiting enticement to join the army and see the world. It was quite probably the only career I could think of that would provide the absence necessary to the narrative of my daydreams. In fact, I did briefly explore the prospect of joining the army when I left Sloane, but that was only because I was at a loss to know what else to do.

Christine's elfin face, framed by her mass of black curls, had stolen my heart from the moment I first laid eyes on her, but there wasn't the slightest sign that the feeling was reciprocated. We didn't last long, Susan Kelly and me. Apart from my unrequited affection for her friend, there was something about Susan's theatrical behaviour that irritated me. I 'packed her in' before the summer had ended. Susan reacted melodramatically, buying Cilla Black's 'You're My World' and delivering it to Colin's house as a present for me, together with a note quoting some of the words.

I suppose I was mean to Susan, but she did get her revenge. A few months after our paths diverged one of her subsequent boyfriends, a big lad from Henry Compton School, challenged me to a fight on the questionable grounds that I'd besmirched Susan Kelly's honour in the way I'd deserted her. He came all the way to the Sloane school gates to throw down his gauntlet.

Rather like the duels fought by aristocrats in the Regency

era, such a challenge, once issued, couldn't be ignored. Susan's boyfriend and I met on a damp night on a patch of grass at the end of Colin's street. There were no 'seconds' and, thankfully, no witnesses as he threw at least three punches to every one of mine, extracting an early submission.

It was all rather noble, really: his defence of his sweetheart's honour, the discretion with which the fight was arranged and his acceptance of my surrender. We even shook hands before parting. No doubt he received a hero's welcome when he returned to Susan.

My increasing interest in girls never distracted me from my passion for music. On the contrary, I was convinced that being in a group, even one as substandard as the Vampires, would make me irresistible to the opposite sex. One morning in the summer holidays, walking to Colin's house from the bus stop for a much-needed Vampires practice session, I saw a crowd of girls congregating outside Pauline Bright's house just along the street.

Colin had a new record that he was desperate for the rest of us to hear. So, at my suggestion, we opened the front-room window, stood around the record-player with our motley collection of instruments and tried to impress the girls outside by pretending it was us playing 'You Really Got Me' by the Kinks. As those fat power chords fizzed from Dave Davies's guitar, it was obvious that we were fooling nobody.

We were as yet unaware that Dave's unique guitar riff had been achieved not only by vastly superior musical skills but with the help of an incision in the speaker cone of his amplifier, technology that the Vampires sadly lacked. Eventually one of Colin's neighbours knocked on the door to complain about the noise. We doubted that ever happened to the Kinks.

By September, 'You Really Got Me' had swept to the top of the charts, boosted by the Kinks' appearance on *Ready, Steady, Go!* and extensive coverage on pirate radio. It also made the US Top 10. The band had been launched only that year, evolving from the Ray Davies Quartet, a group of north London secondary modern schoolboys. There was hope for the Vampires yet.

1965

Like a Rolling Stone

I LEFT SCHOOL in the summer of 1965, a few weeks after my fifteenth birthday. While my time at Sloane Grammar School for Boys had been as unproductive for the school as it was for me, a few of the masters seemed interested in my future. Mr Carlen – the brilliant English teacher who'd nurtured my love of reading and introduced me to the work of C. S. Forester, Geoffrey Household, George Orwell, Wilfred Owen and Arnold Bennett – was aware of my ambition to be 'A Writer'. He even encouraged me to send my adolescent stories and poems to magazines for possible publication. But I was less focused now on writing stories and poems than I was on writing songs and playing the guitar.

Johnny Carter had given me the extraordinarily generous leaving present of a Vox solid electric guitar when I gave up working as his assistant on the milk and paraffin rounds. I was invited to pick my gift from a cellar full of musical instruments in the basement of his house after we'd completed our final delivery together. It seemed that Johnny had yet another occupation, which may not have been entirely legal. All the same, it was largesse indeed. This beautiful instrument came with its own case covered in gingham fabric upon which I transcribed 'The Vampires' with my sister's lipstick. Mike, who managed an electrical shop on the Edgware Road, made me a small amplifier to go with it.

Linda and I had moved south of the Thames to number 11 Pitt House on the Wilberforce estate in York Road, Battersea – a maisonette secured from the council, thanks to the determination of my sister, with the support of our social worker, Mr Pepper.

When Mr Carlen, Mr Pallai, who'd taught us economics and history, and our art master, Mr Marshall, asked Andrew and me what we intended to do with our lives, we romanticised, telling them we were joining a rock group and hoped to be touring the country by the end of the year.

In truth I was going to be a clerk at Remington Electric Shavers in Kensington High Street and Andrew was about to become a butcher. But to be fair, he was becoming an ever more proficient drummer and we did play music together, albeit in the bedroom he shared with his brother.

My guitar hero was Jeff Beck, who'd taken over lead guitar from Eric Clapton in the Yardbirds. I'd seen them play in several venues, including the Marquee club in Wardour Street, progressing from Monday nights at the Hammersmith Palais to sophisticated live music at West End clubs I still wasn't officially old enough to enter.

The Yardbirds were a band so blessed with guitar talent that they had the great Jimmy Page on bass. What thrilled me most about their live performances was the crescendo of noise they built up on songs such as 'I'm a Man'. It involved hitting one chord loudly and rapidly for about thirty seconds. (The most commercial application of this technique would be heard later on David Bowie's 'The Jean Genie'.)

Andrew and I would try to replicate that sound in his house on his quiet estate, to the disgruntlement of his father, who burst into the bedroom one afternoon ordering me to turn my 'jukebox' down (he meant my amplifier) and to stop playing my 'banjo' so loudly. Andrew and I smirked behind his father's back at such clear evidence of how hopelessly 'square' the older generation could be.

I like to think I went from acoustic to electric with Bob Dylan. Ever since he'd entered my life via my sister's new boyfriend, I'd been almost as mesmerised by Dylan as I was by the Beatles. For a short while it seemed as though I was privy to a secret: nobody in Britain, apart from a few folk aficionados, had heard of the singer from Minnesota with the nasal, rough-edged voice. By the time Mike lent me his second album, *The Freewheelin' Bob Dylan*, the songs had become better known than the man who wrote them, thanks mainly to covers by artists such as Peter, Paul and Mary.

It was around 1963, 1964 that the Dylan phenomenon really took off. On the strength of songs like 'The Times They Are a-Changin'', with its thrillingly mutinous line about sons and daughters being 'beyond your command', he began to be talked of in the press as the spokesman for a generation. Suddenly 'protest' songs were in vogue and 'protest singers' were springing up everywhere.

At school we would pore over Dylan's lyrics, reciting them like the poetry we considered them to be. I was inspired to write a pretentious poem, 'The Bomb', which was published in the Sloane school magazine, and even took to wearing a fake leather Dylan cap that had belonged to my sister. Before long even the coolest music show of the day, *Ready, Steady, Go!*, had found a Dylan clone called Donovan to appear on the programme every week.

I persuaded Mike to make me a replica of the contraption that Dylan slung round his neck to hold his harmonica in place. I think he used a wire coat hanger, but his creation not only looked the part, it did the job, and was soon cradling the Höfner 'C' mouth organ into which I blew and sucked without making any noise that was recognisable as music.

In 1965 Dylan shocked the folk fraternity by 'going electric'. Mike bought *Bringing it All Back Home* as soon as it was released, just he did every Dylan album. I think he was as surprised as every other folk fan to find the LP split between electric on one side and acoustic on the other. That was as nothing to the controversy at the Newport Folk Festival in July, when Dylan apparently made a last-minute decision to perform the songs from his new album accompanied not only by a band, which included Mike Bloomfield on guitar and Al Kooper on organ, but by an electric guitar.

Boos from the audience can be distinctly heard on recordings of the event, though whether they were due to the disgruntlement of purists, the shortness of the set or sound-quality problems remains a matter of dispute to this day. Dylan did not appear again at Newport for thirty-seven years, and when he did he was sporting a wig and false beard, perceived by some as an oblique comment on the furore.

I loved everything about that album, from its carefully

crafted cover photograph – Dylan stroking a black cat in a grand-looking room, with a woman in a glamorous red dress, smoking a cigarette, reclining in the background (which in itself suggested that he'd left folk's simplicity behind) – to the glorious electric tracks ('She Belongs to Me', 'Love Minus Zero') and the acoustic masterpieces, 'Mr Tambourine Man' and 'It's Alright Ma (I'm Only Bleeding)'.

For me that album, and the extraordinary single that came later in 1965, 'Like a Rolling Stone', represented the zenith of Dylan's career. I found it hard to like anything he recorded subsequently. His mysterious motorbike accident the following year led to a break in his career and a withdrawal from the public gaze – he did not appear live again until 1968 and there were no tours for nearly eight years. I am very firmly a pre-motorbike-accident Dylan fan. Even his voice had changed when he came back and nothing he produced afterwards would for me ever match the glory of those 1965 releases.

My own mouth organ, 'banjo' and 'jukebox' continued to reside mostly at Andrew's house, with their player dividing his time between there and Colin James's cellar. After my mother's death both families were incredibly kind. I spent Christmas Day 1964 at Andrew's, where his father cooked a huge dinner, taking round a couple of plates piled high with turkey and all the trimmings to two elderly housebound neighbours and dividing the rest between the two adults and five youngsters gathered round his own kitchen table. As it was a special occasion we were allowed into the front room after dinner and I was given a glass of crème-de-menthe, which, Andrew's dad assured me, would dispel the uncomfortable (and rare) feeling of having eaten too much.

Over at Parsons Green, the more well-to-do, more middle-class Jameses for some reason saw me as a moderating influence on their rebellious son. I remember once watching Colin having a stand-up fight with Mr James while I waited for him on the doorstep. They pushed and shoved each other all the way down the hall, arguing over the time Colin was expected to be home. As we walked off together – or stalked off, in Colin's case – his father, dishevelled by the altercation, called after me: 'Try to talk some sense into him, Alan.'

I was keen to repay the kindness Colin's parents had shown me in any way I could, but their son's behaviour was beyond my influence. Not that Colin was wayward enough to leave school when I did that year. He stayed on to do his O-Levels. For Colin, the son of university graduates, it would have been inconceivable not to pursue a place at university, whereas it was a prospect that had never entered my head.

Colin's parents were tolerant and liberal in attitude and I struggled to understand precisely what my friend was rebelling against. The previous summer Mr and Mrs James had been perfectly relaxed when Colin and I, both barely fourteen years of age, had decided to spend ten days hitchhiking round the south coast.

We had set off one morning, our rucksacks packed with snacks lovingly prepared by Mrs James, to walk from Fulham to Hammersmith before managing to hitch our way as far as Berkshire by nightfall. It was pouring with rain and hard to see what we were doing as we pitched Colin's little tent in the countryside.

When we tried to extract the snacks that Colin's mum had prepared we discovered that the zip of the compartment they were stored in had stuck solid. So we had nothing to eat. Completely without experience as campers, we also managed to 'touch' the inside of the roof of the tent (this scraped off some of the lining's waterproof protection, apparently), the rain gradually found its way through and we woke up next morning in damp sleeping bags.

Upon opening the tent flap and stepping outside into the morning light, we realised we'd set up camp not in a bucolic Berkshire meadow as we'd thought, but on the Sunningdale golf course in Ascot. And right now there was a platoon of golfers heading our way.

We made ourselves scarce and off we hitched, heading for Southsea, where we slept on the beach before catching the early-morning ferry to Hayling Island. There we stayed in our leaky tent for five days before Colin pleaded with his parents to send us the train fare home.

Ultimately, it was his mother's tender concern for me that ended my friendship with Colin. I never saw either of my best friends' mothers as being in any way in loco parentis. Indeed, I have to confess that my thoughts towards Mrs James were not entirely pure. Like the French nurse, Mandy Rice-Davies and Kathleen Kelly, Mrs James was the object of my adolescent infatuation. She would have been in her mid-thirties, another redhead and had a lovely alabaster skin. I was entranced by her elegance and impressed by her easy sophistication. Most of all, she was such fun to be with.

Did I ever even know her first name? I doubt it. Raised as I was to be polite and respectful, to me Colin's mum was always Mrs James, just as Andrew's was Mrs Wiltshire.

In the summer of 1965, when Mr and Mrs James invited me

to join the family for a fortnight at Pontin's in Bracklesham Bay near Chichester, I had yet to read *In Praise of Older Women*, Stephen Vizinczey's fictionalised memoir of a young man's erotic misadventures, or to see *The Graduate*. Indeed, Vizinczey's book was still to be published in the UK and Mike Nichols' film had still to be made as we all set off in the Rover Mr James had washed and polished for the occasion.

At the holiday camp, Colin and I soon fell in with a couple of older boys. One of them, our ringleader, was a film projectionist, a job that seemed impossibly romantic to a schoolboy and a clerk at Remington's. We spent a week being taught more than we ever knew about chatting up girls by the two Lotharios we'd befriended. The projectionist was no looker, but he certainly knew how to use what he had, including his occupation, to maximum effect.

With a chalet to ourselves, Colin and I were having a whale of a time, encountering his parents and the four younger children only at the regimented mealtimes, when we had to sit in the places allocated to us at the start of our holiday at a long table shared with other families.

At the end of the first week our two ladykillers left, as did the girls we'd become friends with. We still had another week to go, but it felt as if our holiday was over as well. Unable to join any wider social circle without the patronage of our mentors, we were forced to keep company with Colin's family every evening in the cavernous bar, where at least there was a DJ playing all the latest records. The big summer hit was 'I Got You Babe' by Sonny and Cher, which was aired frequently by popular demand. Every time it came on the dance floor filled with couples taking the male and female roles, the inhibitions of the adults diminishing with every fresh round of drinks.

A camp photographer (by which I mean a photographer based at the camp, rather than one who was camp) snapped away at the dance floor as he had at every Pontin's event throughout our stay. On the Friday, before the churn of arrivals and departures the following day, his pictures would be displayed in the dining room, where they could be purchased to supplement the amateurish photos taken on the family Kodak.

One evening Mrs James had insisted that I join her on the dance floor as Sonny to her Cher. The photographer had captured the moment and on our last Friday, the picture was among several of the James family in various poses displayed for sale. As we trooped out from breakfast Mrs James examined the montage and decided to buy only one: the photograph of her and me masquerading as Sonny and Cher.

This deeply offended Colin, who voiced his disapproval of her choice loudly and belligerently as we queued with his mother to pay.

'Don't be silly, dear,' soothed Mrs James sweetly. 'I've got hundreds of photographs of the rest of us. It would be nice to have one with Alan in it.' I was chuffed, but trying hard not to beam with satisfaction, aware that this might tip Colin over the edge. For he was inconsolable, and sat hunched in a silent sulk all the way back to Fulham.

I lacked the sensitivity to empathise with Colin, who must have been in a stew of complex filial feelings, and resented the way he'd ruined a happy holiday. I was also acutely embarrassed by the whole episode. I resolved never again to allow myself to be cast in the role of an outsider upsetting the equilibrium of a family. Mortified, I severed all ties with Colin and his lovely mother. It was the end of the Vampires.

~

I had no particular thoughts of a long-term career at Remington Electric Shavers. Before leaving school, having quickly decided against the army, I'd been sent to an office in the Fulham Road which dispensed careers advice to kids in my position.

A kindly chap had spent half an hour with me after carefully noting my desire to be 'a writer'. I'd assumed he'd dismiss this romantic notion out of hand, but he did his best to help, suggesting he might be able to find me work writing the blurbs on the backs of paperback novels summarising the plot, or on the sleeves of LP records giving an introduction to the music and the musicians.

It came to nothing, of course. I had no educational qualifications and I imagine I would have needed O-Level English, at least, even to stand a chance of becoming a copywriter.

The kindly chap asked me what else might appeal but beyond my craving to be a pop star, which he couldn't help me with, I didn't have a clue. As a child I'd nursed a vision of living a peripatetic adulthood, driving a Dormobile around the country with a faithful sheepdog as my companion.

I'd probably listened too much to 'Old Shep'. Linda and I had that track on an EP and Elvis always had me in floods of tears when he sang the mournful last line: 'But if dogs have a heaven there's one thing I know, Old Shep has a wonderful home.'

Now that puberty held me in its sweaty embrace this vision had faded. It was a girl I wanted as a companion, not a bloody sheepdog. And it was music I wanted to pursue, so the only itinerant lifestyle that enthused me was one that involved travelling from gig to gig.

In one sense I'd succeeded in my childhood ambition to be nomadic, albeit within the confines of London. From my hub, the flat I shared with Linda at Pitt House on the Wilberforce estate in Battersea, the spokes would take me to South Kensington for work; to Andrew's in Shepherd's Bush and our mutual pal John Williams's place in Acton; to the Churchill estate in Westminster, home to two other mates from Sloane, Philip Yerby and Clive Llewellyn. Though Colin James was now, sadly, off the itinerary, I still tramped to Fulham to see Yvonne Stacey, with whom I remained firm friends.

There were sorties to the West End, to the Marquee in Wardour Street; to the 100 club in Oxford Street to see the Pretty Things; to the Wimbledon Palais for the Rolling Stones and the Crawdaddy club in Richmond for Gary Farr and the T-Bones.

I was an expert on London's bus routes and Harry Beck's elegantly designed map of the Underground. Arrangements were made, meetings co-ordinated, timings synchronised – all without the aid of a landline, let alone a mobile phone or the internet.

Andrew and I would also sometimes go to BBC television recordings, either at the newly built BBC Television Centre, whose construction I had watched on my journeys to QPR's football ground, which was virtually next door, or at their theatre in Shepherd's Bush. The BBC drew its workforce from the local area, including Andrew's estate (his house in Nascot Street was just off Wood Lane, where the landmark new television centre was situated), and his next-door neighbour, who was a cameraman, would give us tickets. I remember being part of the live audience for *Juke Box Jury* and *The Kathy Kirby Show.*

There was one other place I visited in 1965: the home of my girlfriend, Ann. But I can't for the life of me recall exactly where she lived. It was in the vast, unexplored connurbation of north London, uncharted territory for me. All I remember is that I would leave Remington's at 5pm, catch a bus round the corner in Church Street and arrive at a bus stop outside Ann's house almost an hour later. The distance involved in pursuing the relationship was probably the main reason why we weren't together for very long.

I can't even recall now how we met, but I think it was on one of my forays into the West End. Ann was lovely. A little older than me, she was slim with very short auburn hair and a smile that lit her almond eyes. She worked in a shop and lived with her mother in a suite of nice rooms at the top of a large, multi-occupied house.

The three of us would sit in the kitchen and eat the splendid tea that Ann's mother prepared for every one of my half-dozen visits. Then Ann and I would go to her room to 'play records'. Oh, the excitement we shared behind that unlocked door. Ann's mother trusted that my intentions towards her daughter were virtuous. She was wrong. But even if they had been, Ann's intentions towards me weren't entirely innocent.

We certainly played records, stacking ten 45s on to the thin metal spindle and swinging across the arm that held them in place like parachutists waiting to jump. One by one they dispensed their two and a half minutes of joy – Dusty and Sandie, Manfred Mann and the Walker Brothers, the Supremes and the

Four Tops. We were enraptured not so much by the music as by each other, a new experience for me. Once those records began their descent we had a little over twenty minutes of sweet and tender discovery before the record-player had to be restacked. Ann's mother never came into the room, but sometimes in the silence that fell while we changed records, she'd call to us from the kitchen door, asking us if we'd like a cup of tea. We always declined.

I was never subjected to a lesson at school that could be even loosely described as sex education. It was in Ann's snug little bedroom that I learned everything I needed to know about the erotic pleasure of how to 'play records'.

∽

I received two invitations to Christmas dinner that year – three if you count the standing one to join Linda at Mike's family home in Watford.

By now my sister was engaged to be married (more seriously than she had been with Jimmy Carter). While I was delighted that Mike was going to be my brother-in-law, I had no wish to spend Christmas with his elderly parents under the supervision of my sister.

Linda was away in Watford every weekend and during the week we hardly saw each other. We were both at work all day – Linda in Hammersmith, where she was a nursery nurse – and my busy social life and her courtship monopolised our free time. Being alone in the flat felt entirely natural and, as a working man aged fifteen and a half, I cherished the freedom my friends so envied.

So I awoke alone in 11 Pitt House on Christmas morning 1965 before setting off on foot down York Road to Wandsworth Bridge and across the Thames as the pale December light cast its reflection on the mud-dark water. There was the usual powerful, immutable aroma emanating from the Booth's gin distillery, but I'd grown so used to it that only its absence would have been noticeable.

I was wearing a brand-new pair of desert boots, a Mod favourite, that Linda had left as my present. These fashionable, sand-coloured, mock-suede beauties were taking me to Yvonne Stacey's, where I'd been invited for lunch. Yvonne's German mother – a wonderful, richly eccentric character who brought a dash of colour to the semi-suburban normality of London SW6 – was deeply interested in art and literature. Because I read a lot of books, Mrs Stacey considered me to be a fellow cognoscente. It had been several months since she'd lent me her copy of Dante's *Inferno*, and I knew she'd be looking forward to discussing it with me after lunch. I had yet to read a word of Dante but I had an escape plan in place. Immediately after the meal, Yvonne was intending to visit her boyfriend. I would take advantage of the natural break in proceedings to make sure I left with her, explaining that I did not want to be late for my next engagement.

I'd been invited to spend the evening with John Williams at his parents' neat, semi-detached council house on the Wormholt estate in Acton.

There must have been some kind of rudimentary Christmas Day public transport then because I managed to get to Acton by late afternoon, in time for a salad tea and an evening listening to records in John's room with his friend Wendy, a quiet, dreamy girl with little in the way of conversation.

As we lounged about, John and I indulging in the odd bit of desultory chatter, he produced one of his presents, the newly released debut album of a local band called the Who.

It was a good album with two outstanding tracks. I've always regarded 'The Kids Are Alright' as an anthemic tribute to west London Mods. Whether that was Pete Townshend's intention I have no idea, but the Who were undoubtedly a Mod band. The previous year they had even performed for a few months, and released a single, under a different name, the High Numbers – Mod slang for the upper echelon of admired and superior Mods. Whatever the case, the track 'caught the moment' as well as being a cracking tune.

'My Generation' was something else altogether. It was quite simply astonishing. Its pounding bass opening, the manic drumming, stuttering vocals, big climactic chords . . . Lolling around in John Williams's bedroom, I was aware that I was hearing something uniquely powerful. While 'I hope I die before I get old' was a slogan I wasn't quite prepared to march behind, it captured the raw explosion of youth culture and the determination of us baby-boomers to defend it against the attacks of an older generation who simply didn't understand it.

If Bob Dylan was our gentle poet, 'My Generation' was our battering ram.

1966

Summer in the City

ON 24 SEPTEMBER 1966 my sister Linda married Mike Whitaker in Watford. They had already taken out a mortgage on a house in St James Road, a few doors down from Linda's in-laws.

I attended the wedding wearing a cotton Madras jacket, my long, wavy hair flowing free (or 'in a mess', as Linda tartly observed). Guests included some of the Coxes, the family of my boyhood friend Tony, whose mother Pat had been close to Lily, Andrew Wiltshire and a sprinkling of relatives from Liverpool, among them my cousin Pam, whom Andrew spent the entire evening trying to chat up.

We drank and talked and danced, to the Stones, to Dave, Dee, Dozy, Beaky, Mick and Tich; to the Easybeats, an Australian band whose single 'Friday on My Mind' had just been released, to great acclaim from me and my sister. When there was a good-natured protest by the older guests, who demanded something more agreeable to them, Ken Dodd and Jim Reeves forced their way on to the turntable, to the groans of the youngsters.

I was a complete poseur, trying to combine the serious de-meanour of Scott Walker with the panache of Stevie Marriott, the Mod style icon and leader of my latest favourite band, the Small Faces.

For my sister and me, the wedding marked the end of the life we'd shared since my birth. Mr Pepper, the social worker responsible for keeping us together and out of 'care' after the death of our mother, had obviously decided that I was safe in Linda's hands. At any rate, his visits had reduced considerably during our two years in Battersea, and we saw nothing of him after Linda married.

She tried to convince me to move with her to Watford, where there were three bedrooms in the 'semi' she was so proud of. But to me Watford represented the far north and I was resistant to all attempts to prise me out of London.

Linda and I have never ceased to worship Mr Pepper and to hold his profession in the utmost respect. He was the only per-son 'in authority' we encountered throughout our eventful childhood. Or perhaps it would be more accurate to say he was the only one I encountered, as Linda must have dealt with many more than I knew about. It was solely because he listened to Linda and acted on his instincts rather than rigidly follow-ing the rulebook that we were able to stay together. We still speak fondly to this day of Mr Pepper, and how it was he who ensured our future happiness. Linda even invited him to her wedding, but he wouldn't come.

I'm not sure how Mr Pepper would have felt about my esca-pades in Soho with Andrew. The wedding marked the end of a wonderful, hot summer in which the two of us headed most weekends into the West End, often with no bigger plans than to walk the streets absorbing the atmosphere. Given the risk he'd taken by not placing me with foster parents, Mr Pepper would probably have lost his job if things had gone wrong.

He needn't have worried. We weren't the slightest bit interested in drugs, and drugs didn't seem to be the slightest bit interested in us. Apart from somebody once offering us purple hearts at the Hammersmith Palais when we were schoolboys, we never came across a drug-pusher and no drugs were ever pushed our way.

I suspect that, for all the talk of a generation turning on, tuning in and dropping out in the sixties, tripping on LSD was a middle-class preoccupation and there was more chance of being pressurised into taking drugs on a university campus than on the Wilberforce estate. In any case, you needed money to buy drugs, and we were constantly broke.

I'd left Remington's for Tesco in January, upping my income with a job as assistant warehouse manager at the supermarket in King Street in Hammersmith. They paid me £8 a week rather than the £10 a fortnight I'd been paid at Remington. But still, after helping Linda with the rent and saving up to buy the Ben Sherman and Fred Perry shirts I favoured, I was left with very little disposable income (or spare cash, as we called it then).

Fortunately, the man who delivered Nevill's bread to Tesco every morning carried a stash of contraband EMI LPs. His name was Fred and he had a dark, immaculately shaped moustache which sat above his upper lip like a blackbird in flight. My first task of the day was to give him a hand in with the trays of sliced loaves. Fred was a fellow QPR fan and we'd chew the cud for a while about football before Fred dropped his voice to a murmur and listed the albums he had on board for half the shop price.

It was from Fred that I acquired *Revolver*, the musical highlight of that or, come to think of it, any other summer. Still my favourite Beatles album, *Revolver* achieved what I hadn't believed attainable: it was better than its predecessor, *Rubber Soul*.

The title was a clever pun on the way we listened to music at the time: putting a slab of vinyl the size of a large pizza on to a turntable, applying a needle and listening as it moved through the five or six tracks on that side. And what wonderful sounds emitted from *Revolver*. Familiarity has made it impossible to recapture the initial impact of songs such as 'Eleanor Rigby', 'And Your Bird Can Sing', 'I'm Only Sleeping' and 'Tomorrow Never Knows'. The ability of the Beatles to continue to break new ground musically, and for it all to work so brilliantly, was breathtaking.

I took *Revolver* home and listened to it alone in the flat. There were times when, in an effort to imagine myself as Paul McCartney, I'd mime to his songs in front of the huge mirror over the mantelpiece, with Linda's old school hockey stick standing in for Paul's Höfner violin bass. I even held it left-handed for accuracy.

The hockey stick doubled as a weapon for protecting ourselves against burglars. There was no security on outer entrances to blocks of flats in those days. Anyone could mount the stairs to our landing. And there was some hostility to Linda and me among several of our neighbours, who felt it was wrong for two teenagers to be allocated a council flat when whole families remained on the waiting list. We suspected that the three break-ins we suffered during our tenancy were orchestrated by the big lump of a lad who lived next door with his parents. We were always away when these burglaries took place, which heightened our suspicions.

The hockey stick was never stolen but they took my Vox solid electric guitar and, on their second visit, our old Dansette record-player, which upset me more than losing the Vox because of its sentimental value. For some reason they never took our records, which made us feel almost offended, as it seemed to be a slur on our musical tastes. Neither did they remove our rented telly, which was strange, given that they nicked all the other electrical goods we possessed.

The Wilberforce estate wasn't what we would have classified as 'rough'. There wasn't the constant domestic violence of our childhood in Southam Street – or, if there was, it was better hidden. And I didn't feel threatened by the local kids who played football in the space between the blocks of flats and ignored my comings and goings.

You did have to adopt the demeanour of the streets: a kind of swagger in the walk, a narrowing of the eyes, a forceful way of dragging on a cigarette or aggressively chewing a piece of gum. This posturing and the requisite accessories had been an essential precaution for a boy growing up in North Kensington and they continued to serve me well now. Up to a point.

That point was reached not on the mean streets where I'd grown up, or even on the Wilberforce estate, but on the Churchill estate in Pimlico. Yes, in Westminster, London SW1. Bloody Pimlico!

One Sunday in 1966 I'd gone there to see my old school-friend Philip Yerby. I also had a love interest on the Churchill estate, a girl named Janice McDonald, whom I'd met through Philip. He and I were walking across the estate on this quiet Sunday lunchtime, heading for Janice's flat. We never made it.

It was pouring with rain and we were hunched beneath an umbrella Philip had borrowed from his mum when we passed two older boys coming in the other direction. It must have been the umbrella that interfered with our defence mechanisms. It's difficult to look hard while holding a brolly, and the very fact that we were using one at all must have marked us out as legitimate targets.

We took no notice of these boys as we walked by them, no words were said, no glances exchanged. But about a hundred yards further on we heard running feet behind us and as I turned to check what was happening a fist hit me full in the mouth.

Staggering around spitting out blood and teeth, I saw that Philip was on the pavement being mercilessly kicked by a second attacker as my assailant weighed up whether to come at me again. He'd probably hurt his hand on my mouth and decided he'd done me enough damage. The two of them ran off, whereupon, to my amazement, Philip leaped to his feet unharmed. By adopting the foetal position, with his arms covering his head, he'd managed to protect himself.

I had not been so lucky. Philip had the good sense to take me straight to Westminster Hospital in Horseferry Road. A dentist saw me immediately and asked Philip to return to the scene of the crime, find my three missing teeth and run back with them. He then proceeded to replant them into my gums, securing them in place with a scaffolding of wires which I had to endure for many months.

Forty-three years later, when I became home secretary, my press secretary informed me one day that a photo-op had been arranged for me, walking the streets with a neighbourhood police team accompanied by the deputy commissioner of the Metropolitan Police.

When I asked her where we were going for this media jamboree, she replied distractedly, 'Oh, not far. It's on the Churchill estate in Pimlico.'

As the assembled hordes of cameramen snapped away at the deputy commissioner and me surrounded by coppers, I resisted the temptation to ask the obvious question: 'Where were you lot when I needed you?'

~

I grafted my way through 1966 in the Tesco warehouse, sweeping, tidying, unloading vans and storing the produce in its allocated place on the warehouse floor. It was there that I learned the art of wielding my broom to vanquish the constantly accumulating dust and dirt. I also learned the skill of flattening cardboard boxes and feeding them into a mechanical press with a huge iron weight that was ratcheted down like some instrument of medieval torture until the cardboard was reduced to a tight parcel which could be bound with twine ready for disposal.

When there was nothing to do in the warehouse I'd have to stack shelves, and on the occasional Saturday morning, when it was all hands to the pump, I'd work on the tills. Being on the supermarket checkout back then was very different from the slick operation it is today.

There was no barcode technology. Every item had to be priced by hand; every tube of toothpaste or tin of peaches had its little stick-on price tag. The shelf-stackers used a special hand-held device to label everything they put on the shelves – and to label it all again as rampant inflation led to price increases on what seemed like a monthly basis.

Long queues would form at the checkouts, particularly during the peak shopping period of Saturday mornings, when I'd be drafted in as an extra pair of hands. I wasn't as quick as the regular checkout staff, taking more time to find the price and punch it on to the round buttons on the till. Decimalisation was still several years away, so all the prices were in pounds, shillings and pence, with the odd halfpenny thrown in. Nobody seemed to mind queuing. I suppose it was the norm then, and in any case, waiting at a busy grocer's shop where there was no self-service would have taken much longer.

With no credit or debit cards, every customer paid in cash and most of them spent ages fumbling in purses or pockets for the right change. Then there were Green Shield stamps to be handed out, according to how much had been spent. These were an early version of today's reward schemes, but a lot more fiddly. Customers had to stick them into stamp books acquired for the purpose, which could be saved up and exchanged for a range of goods from a catalogue. It was stressful, but sitting at the checkouts was a welcome relief from the warehouse and it gave me the opportunity to take the weight off my feet.

I worked at Tesco through a blistering summer full of

fabulous music, none of which wafted out of the speakers dotted around the store. From these came the mushy sound of something that was supposed to be music but never quite fitted the description, like margarine passing itself off as butter. Sold specifically to be played in shops, its brand name eventually became a generic term we all recognise: muzak. The only relief came when one of the staff broke into the transmission to proclaim a special offer: 'In aisle number four, cans of Batchelors marrowfat peas are half-price for one week only. Thank you for shopping at Tesco.'

In the warehouse my manager, Ronnie Handley, had his own radio tuned to the pirate stations that continued to feed our appetite for pop by blasting out records from early in the morning until late at night while the BBC Light Programme remained frustrated by the restrictions of the 'needle time' agreement with the Musicians' Union. The pirates were going from strength to strength. By now they had built up a listenership of between 10 and 15 million. It was thanks to these broadcasters lying just beyond the reach of the law, and the two flagship television shows, ITV's *Ready, Steady, Go!* and the BBC's *Top of the Pops*, that young people were able to follow the transformation of popular music.

America had absorbed the influences of the British musical invasion they had seen a few years before and US bands were now setting new standards. So much new and exciting music reverberated through 1966. Earlier in the year I'd acquired *Pet Sounds* from Fred the bread man. Brian Wilson, the Beach Boys' reclusive leader, apparently produced this sophisticated album in response to the Beatles' *Rubber Soul*. Interestingly, at first it was better received in the UK, where it was an instant critical and commercial success, than it was in the US. I loved 'Wouldn't it Be Nice', the first track on *Pet Sounds*, and the aforementioned 'Friday on My Mind' by the Easybeats, but my song of '66 was one by a US band called the Lovin' Spoonful.

While the Beach Boys were all about sun-kissed days on a Californian coast that existed for me only in my imagination, 'Summer in the City' was gloriously urban, tapping into my own experience of Andrew and me traipsing around Soho 'hotter than a match head', the backs of our necks getting dirty and gritty, wishing that there was a rooftop at our disposal where, like John Sebastian, the Lovin' Spoonful's songwriter, we could find the cooler evening air.

Andrew had joined me at Tesco, in the butchery department, where he plied his trade in a section of the warehouse. It would be many years before butchers went front of house in British supermarkets. As for delicatessens, international cuisine remained so alien to our palates that olive oil, traditionally used in Britain as a remedy for earache, was still available from chemists on prescription.

Unfortunately for Andrew, he worked a full six-day week whereas I had Saturday afternoons off, in lieu of the extra hours I worked on Monday and Tuesday evenings when most of the produce arrived for warehousing. So it was that on Saturday, 30 July, I returned alone to Pitt House to watch England beat West Germany in the World Cup final at Wembley, picking stale custard creams out of a biscuit tin as the match went into extra time.

Andrew would not usually have cared about missing a match. He had no interest in football. But this was more than a football game: it was a national event that everybody wanted to be part of. Not only was a World Cup final being played on our home turf, but we were in it. And, of course, we won.

That night the two of us went up west and jostled among the crowds cramming Trafalgar Square. The surrounding roads and pavements were gridlocked. A concert of car horns filled the warm summer air of the country that was now champion of the world. Honk, honk, honk honk honk, honk honk honk honk, 'ENGLAND!'

We stood with hundreds of others on the plinth of Nelson's Column, shouting our refrain, shaking hands with strangers and trying to chat up unaccompanied girls. Afterwards we walked all the way back to Pitt House, as we'd done so often. This time we felt we'd had a small taste of what our parents must have experienced on VE Day. Our boys had beaten the Germans 4–2 to take the Jules Rimet trophy for the first (and, so far, only) time.

We both had girlfriends that summer, although they weren't with us that night for some reason. Conveniently for us, and perhaps for them, we were going out with two sisters, Stephanie and Deborah Blake. 'Steph' and 'Debs' lived with their parents in a prefab on the White City estate off South Africa Road. These pre-constructed houses were erected all over the country after the war as a temporary measure to address the housing shortage caused by Hitler's bombs. They were only designed to last for about ten years, but many of them survived a lot longer. Some are still housing families today.

Mrs Blake was always ill. Looking back, I think she may have been an alcoholic, though I had no concept then of what an alcoholic was. Mr Blake, to me, represented the best of adult masculinity. He had a tough, stern demeanour but was so gentle in the way he treated his fragile wife and so considerate to his daughters and their friends. He talked to us as if we were the grown-ups we thought we were and I valued his approval.

The sisters followed an etiquette handed down to working-class girls through the generations. They would never enter a pub unaccompanied or smoke or whistle or chew gum in the street. When walking with a boy, they always had to be on the inside (apparently, so that if a car accidentally mounted the pavement, the boy would manfully shield them from the impact). To transgress these rules was to be considered 'common'. There was a long list of dos and don'ts to be followed in public, but in the privacy of 11 Pitt House there were few inhibitions.

I fell madly in love with Stephanie Blake, only to be spurned for an older rival. When she packed me in she at least had the good grace to do it to my face, gazing at me sympathetically with her lovely dark eyes as she broke the news that she wanted somebody more mature. Which was fine, except that the guy she dumped me for was her cousin.

I wrote a melancholy song, 'Stephanie's Blues', to express my heartache.

> But when you love you soon forget
> The pain your love may cause, and yet,
> You bear; a lover is a fool.

As if this wasn't pathetic enough, I imagined myself busking in rags, singing Bob Dylan songs on Shepherd's Bush Green, where Stephanie was bound to see me. I pictured her bursting into tears at the pain she'd inflicted and the love she'd discarded.

In an act of solidarity, Andrew finished with Deborah. But a change in our lives was imminent that would be even more important to us than loves won and lost. At the end of 1966 a tiny asteroid entered the musical universe: our first proper band, the Area, was formed.

1967

Hard Life

ANDREW AND I could never have formed a band by ourselves. Two sixteen-year-olds with few resources and not much resourcefulness, we needed help. By then we were properly equipped instrumentally. Andrew had a drum kit purchased by his parents, bit by bit, as Christmas and birthday presents, and I had a new guitar, acquired through a posthumous intervention by my mother.

As I bemoaned my stolen Vox, Linda revealed that Lily had somehow squirrelled away £40 in a Post Office savings account as a bequest to her children. When my sister discovered the account after Lily's death, she had decided to save it and give it all to me on my eighteenth birthday. Just before her wedding, and our parting of the ways, she told me of this legacy and gave me the option of having it now, two years earlier than she'd planned, to buy a new guitar.

It was an act of providence, as if Lily had reached from beyond the grave to bestow on me the thing I wanted most in life. Wandering around Soho I'd seen it in the window of a musical instrument shop in Wardour Street – my dream guitar: a cherry-red Höfner Verithin with Venetian double cutaways, mother-of-pearl inlay on the head and neck, a black scratchboard and a Bigsby tremolo unit.

It was called a Verithin because it was, well, very thin – about an inch and a quarter, about as slim as a semi-acoustic guitar could be. It was second hand (they'd stopped making them in the early sixties), but that was what I wanted: a guitar that had seen active service. The price was £35, including a red, cheese-wedge-shaped case.

The only guitar I might have swapped it for was a Fender Telecaster, but I didn't see one of those for sale and besides, they were not as beautiful as the Verithin. My guitar hero Jeff Beck had been playing a Fender Telecaster when Andrew and I saw him at the Marquee Club early in 1967, just after he launched the Jeff Beck Group. I remember, as we discussed the band's brilliant, gravel-voiced singer, Rod Stewart, well known in Soho as Rod the Mod, a guy next to us commenting that he had missed his chance of the big time and would always be confined to the club circuit.

By then the Area had been born. Its architect had arrived on the scene in the summer of 1966 in the shape of Danny Curtis. Danny was the boyfriend of Carole Cox, Tony Cox's sister, who had been a friend of Linda's at Bevington School, and lived opposite the Cox family in Lancaster Road in North Kensington. He had been going steady with Carole for some years – not strictly speaking the boy next door, but the boy across the road.

One evening, Danny had come over to Pitt House with a serious proposition. He badly wanted to be a singer in a band and suggested that and Andrew and I join him as the core of a five-piece outfit. He would place an advert in *Melody Maker* to recruit a bass and a lead guitar. He would be the manager – our Andrew Loog Oldham as well as our Mick Jagger. He would also get the bookings, drive us around in his battered Bedford van, arrange rehearsals and distribute the money we earned.

Danny Curtis was a proper grown-up, pushing twenty, and as streetwise as anybody we'd ever met. Stick-thin, fashionably slightly built and with a mop of straight blond hair, he might not have been blessed with any great musical talent, but he certainly had the gift of the gab. He could talk his way into (and out of) anything. His voice was passable, and what he lacked in vocal dexterity he more than made up for with his sheer stage presence.

The idea was quickly sold. Danny's energy was infectious and his dedication to the project total and sincere. The three of us decided on a name. I'm pretty sure the Area was my suggestion, in homage to the basement domains of the crumbling houses in Southam Street that were known as 'areas'.

As it happened, I was about to become a neighbour of Danny's. When Linda returned the keys of our flat to the council to begin her married life, I was going to have to leave Battersea. With all attempts to persuade me to move to Watford having failed, she reluctantly acquiesced to an approach being made to Mrs Cox, at whose home I'd been billeted in the final days of Lily's life when Linda was almost permanently resident at Hammersmith Hospital.

So I returned to my manor, back to the familiar territory of Bramley Road, Ladbroke Grove and the Portobello market. To a household of affection and generosity, of proper cooked breakfasts and warm, paraffin-heated rooms. The Coxes' home in Lancaster Road was round the corner from Latimer Road tube station and I was reunited with the Metropolitan Line and the tube network that was so sadly lacking south of the Thames. Andrew was once again within walking distance and the manager and lead singer of our new band conveniently just over the road.

On the surface, not much had changed in North Kensington in the two years I'd been away. Southam Street had emptied and a few more slum houses had vanished. But there was an unease in the air. The children of the first wave of immigrants, who had grown up witnessing the way their parents had been treated by some of their neighbours and by the police, were determined not to tolerate such treatment themselves. But while racism and tension remained rife, steps were also being taken to bring the community together.

The first event that would evolve into the Notting Hill carnival, a street party for local children designed to encourage cultural unity, had taken place that summer, metamorphosing into a carnival procession when a steel band decided to take their music around the neighbourhood. Snatches of calypso and reggae could now be heard on the streets, elements of Caribbean style were making their mark on the Mod movement, the groundwork for a mutual understanding was being laid and the seeds of new influences on British music were being sown. The capability of music to help unite people was beginning to have an effect.

Pat and Albert Cox rented two floors of a house from a private landlord. Along with practically every family in the vicinity, they were waiting for the offer of a council house where their children could all have their own room. Mrs Cox managed to squeeze an extra bed into the room shared by her two sons, Tony and Paul. Although it was a long while since Tony and I had been the inseparable duo of our primary-school days, we had a perfectly amicable relationship and I often rode around on the back of his Lambretta. Paul, who was the youngest by some distance, was just reaching secondary-school age and was understandably miffed at having a third person imposed on him in a bedroom barely big enough for two. At the time, though, his antipathy hardly registered with me. He was a little kid who wasn't going to stop me settling into the familial bliss of my new home.

Carole, as the only girl, had the luxury of her own room, but with no bathroom, she had to use the kitchen sink to wash like the rest of us. The mornings were very regimented, with everyone off to work or school, but fortunately we boys didn't need quite as long at the sink as Carole did.

By the time I was back in North Kensington, towards the end of that unforgettable summer of 1966, the Area was up and running. The *Melody Maker* advert had come up trumps, and by October two guys in their late teens, Tony Kearns and Ian Clark, had expanded us from a trio into a quintet. Tony had recently moved down from Chester with his exotic Futurama guitar, determined to make it as a musician. Ian was a cerebral Scot who was studying music at a university somewhere in London. He played bass guitar for the Area but was a gifted musician capable of playing many instruments.

Danny found a base for us at the Fourth Feathers youth club close to the Edgware Road. It was there that we practised, stored our equipment and performed in public for the first time. Before long we were playing gigs all over west London and spending most of our Sunday mornings at the Fourth Feathers rehearsing new material. At lunchtime we'd take a break and head round to a local pub, a novel experience for me and Andrew. Licensing laws, like the age restrictions at the Hammersmith Palais, weren't as vigorously applied then and we were never challenged, despite being well under age. We took the precaution of not drawing attention to ourselves: Danny, Tony or Ian always ordered the drinks.

What we didn't appreciate at the time was that we were experiencing the last days of the traditional London boozer. My father would have felt at home in that pub off Praed Street. There was a honky-tonk piano which, to our amazement, Ian took to playing, reeling off popular songs from the forties and fifties. There were no fruit machines or television screens, or any other distractions, save for a dartboard in the public bar and a shove ha'penny game available on request.

There was smoke and noise and great gales of laughter from toothless men and women nursing glasses of Mackeson or light and bitter. They could have walked straight off the set of one of those black-and-white films made during the war where jolly Cockneys rolled out the barrel in defiance of Hitler's bombs. Since this was, of course, only twenty years after the war had ended, many of those who packed the pub on those Sunday lunchtimes may well have been drinking there during the Blitz.

They probably looked upon us as decadent representatives of a mollycoddled generation but we were treated with affectionate good humour, especially after Ian became the impromptu pianist. I remember one gaggle of old dears insisting that my pale baby face must be 'rouged', a suspicion no doubt arising from the firm belief that anyone playing in a 'beat group' must be of questionable sexuality. We would return to our rehearsals after these raucous sessions re-energised, if a little worse for wear.

I learned so much from Ian and Tony about chord progression, keys and harmony. For Andrew and me, the step up from playing as a duo in his bedroom to being part of a proper band, performing on stage to live audiences, was like experiencing the joys of cycling after years of being confined to an indoor exercise bike.

The Area was never anything but a pop group churning out the hits of the time. Our playlist embraced 'Working in the Coal Mine' and 'Time Is on My Side', 'Satisfaction' and 'Hang on Sloopy', 'Hold Tight' and 'Semi-Detached Suburban Mr James'. We never needed to buy sheet music because Ian could always be relied upon to work out the chords. Danny would be on lead vocals for most songs, although I'd take centre stage for the Small Faces' number 'All or Nothing' and the Yardbirds' 'For Your Love'. Danny would tap a tambourine during these intervals, taking a rest from his usual frantic stage performances. He always wore a purple satin shirt with tight white trousers that made him look like an aubergine balanced on a couple of pipe-cleaners.

By early 1967 we felt that we'd established ourselves. The Area had a regular midweek booking at the Pavilion pub in North Pole Road, opposite Wormwood Scrubs, and Danny had the diary filled with Saturday engagements. Our going rate was £7 a booking, which was shared equally, £1 8s each. Even though Danny did all the extra work – not just drumming up the bookings, but transporting the gear, setting it up and dealing with any electrical mishaps – he insisted on everyone being paid the same.

By now I'd left Tesco, having sworn at the manager and marched out in high dudgeon just before Christmas 1966. We'd argued about the state of the warehouse I'd been left to manage on my own after Ronnie Handley left to become a sales rep for Smith's Crisps in October. The resentment I'd been nursing about being given greater responsibility with no pay rise had boiled over when the store manager ordered me to sweep the warehouse just as I was going for my scheduled lunch break. If the case had ever gone to a tribunal, I would have said they had sacked me while Tesco would have claimed I'd resigned. We would both have been right.

As it was, I was out of work for less than a week. Ronnie Handley came to the Coxes' house to tell me that there was a vacancy at a much smaller supermarket, Anthony Jackson's on the Upper Richmond Road in East Sheen. It had a manager and three staff – Kath, Sandra and, from the following Monday morning, me.

As I earned only £10 a week, two gigs with the Area increased my wages by about a third. But money was irrelevant to the pure joy of being in a band. I would have paid for the privilege.

As well as raiding the hit parade for material, Ian and Tony had begun to write their own songs and we'd introduced two of them, 'Hard Life' and 'Control of My Soul', into our playlist. I'd been writing songs myself since I was eight years old, inspired by Lonnie Donegan and the country and western music I heard on the wireless. By now I was writing folksy stuff that didn't lend itself to electrification, apart from a Cat Stevens-type ditty called 'I Have Seen' that we'd also started to include in the set.

Danny was convinced that Ian and Tony had produced a potential chart-topper in 'Hard Life' that would secure our fame and fortune. My song was seen as a half-decent 'B' side. He insisted that we got the songs copyrighted and set about looking for a recording studio where we could cut a demo disc.

What we never expected was that he'd opt for one of the most famous recording studios in the country. Regent Sound was in Denmark Street, famously also known as London's Tin Pan Alley. Like its New York counterpart, this street was the hub of the British music industry, the place where music publishers clustered with their composers, arrangers and musicians. It was where new songs had been rehearsed and acetates recorded going back to the 1920s.

The Regent Sound studio was where the Stones had recorded their debut album, where Jimi Hendrix, the Kinks, the Who, the Troggs, the Yardbirds, Amen Corner, the Bee Gees, and now the Area, committed their genius to vinyl.

I suppose there weren't that many studios for hire in 1967 but there must have been cheaper places than Regent Sound. Danny was a delivery driver earning very little, yet he booked these top-grade facilities entirely at his own expense. We would have one hour, including the time it took to set up our gear and dismantle it afterwards. He may have negotiated a discount, I don't know – Danny certainly knew how to cut a deal. He had already blagged an old Marshall amp from Don Arden, the manager of the Small Faces, a band that also practised occasionally at the Fourth Feathers.

We entered that revered and sacred studio on a cold February night in 1967 and got cracking. 'Hard Life' is a jaunty little song with a call-and-response chorus ('Now it's a hard (hard), hard (hard) life/It would be hard (hard), hard (hard), harder without you ...'). Tony and I sang the 'hard' response to

Danny's call, leading into a two- and then three-part harmony. 'Listen to my song' (Danny on his own); 'Yesterday has gone' (Danny and me); 'Life goes on and oooooon' (Danny, me and Tony).

We did a couple of takes, overlaid the harmonies and then sat in the control room as the engineer played back the finished version. Oh, the thrill of that moment. It wasn't a great song, to be honest, but it was solid pop, with a hook, performed with energy and enthusiasm. What made hearing it that night so amazing was the state-of-the-art sound system.

All the recorded music we'd ever heard up to that moment had poured out of tiny (and tinny) speakers built into the front of record-players, or from radios, fading in and out of frequency in the case of Radio Luxembourg and the pirate stations. Even when the discs we liked made it on to the BBC, what was relayed was an imperfect reproduction accompanied by persistent crackling. We weren't among the minority of more prosperous record collectors who could indulge in 'hi-fi' equipment and it would be years before headphones were widely available.

And so the sound that emerged from the high-quality speakers in that soundproofed studio had an extraordinary purity that was brand new to us. It made our music sound better than it was.

Having taken so much care over 'Hard Life', we were left with barely five minutes to record 'I Have Seen': no time for a run-through, or to overdub the splendid harmonies we'd rehearsed. We had to do it in one take. Danny's voice came in off-key and Ian's bass was plonky, but it would have to do. We were quickly shepherded out of the studio to make way for the next session. It's a poor rendition of 'I Have Seen' but at least it demonstrates Andrew's proficiency. His drumming is easily the best thing about it.

We were handed the reel-to-reel tape of the recording and a few weeks later Danny collected the ten vinyl discs of 'Hard Life/I Have Seen' that we'd had pressed. He then set about trying to get the record companies to listen to our work of art. While I stacked shelves at Anthony Jackson's, Andrew butchered at Tesco, Tony toiled away at his clerical job and Ian studied, Danny arranged meetings with Pye, Philips and a new record label called Deram. I think he also sent one of those precious discs to EMI. Another couple were posted to pirate radio stations but never played.

No deals were done, no contracts signed and our demo disc would be the only record we ever made. *Top of the Pops* would never be troubled by the Area, but we carried on in anticipation of our big chance, having a whale of a time in the process. We played in pubs, church halls, working-men's clubs and youth clubs, at wedding receptions and birthday parties. The previous December, before I left Tesco, we'd performed at their staff Christmas do. In March we played at a dance in Shepherd's Bush on the very evening that QPR, the team most of the guests supported and which I revered, won the League Cup at Wembley. In May we were onstage in front of a thousand people at Aylesbury College as the support band for Fifth Dynasty. Danny told us that Don Arden had mentioned the possibility of us going on tour with the Small Faces. We were sure that it was only a matter of time before the breakthrough came.

Unfortunately, what came wasn't a breakthrough but a break-in. In the autumn of 1967 somebody smashed the locks on the room at the Fourth Feathers where we stored our equipment. They stole everything that was there: Andrew's drum kit, Ian's bass, all our microphones, amplifiers and speakers, plus my newly acquired fuzz-box (a pedal that basically fattened the sound of the note, as in Keith Richards' opening riff on 'Satisfaction').

Thankfully, I'd taken my precious Höfner Verithin in its cheese-wedge case back to the Coxes', so at least that didn't fall into the hands of the thieves, though my newly purchased Marshall amp did. The amp Mike had made me wasn't good enough for live performances with the Area and, as I wasn't old enough to sign a hire-purchase agreement, my boss at Anthony Jackson had acted as guarantor to enable me to buy a bigger one. It was uninsured, so I was left with two years of substantial monthly payments for a piece of equipment I'd never see again.

It was like a bereavement. Andrew was devastated. He'd lost about five years' worth of Christmas and birthday presents. We'd sit mournfully in the Tower Coffee Bar in Hammersmith, where we often met, trying to break the world-record time for making a single cup of coffee last. 'At least you've got your guitar,' he'd observe glumly. 'I've got nothing.'

I refused to accept that it was the end of our dream. Even while playing with the Area, Andrew and I had been surreptitiously pursuing other music opportunities, reading the small ads in the *Melody Maker* assiduously every week. Andrew once applied to be drummer for the Mindbenders, a band notable for the rare feat of going on to greater success once they'd unshackled their name from that of their front man, Wayne Fontana. Their first single after the split, 'Groovy Kind of Love', had been a huge hit around the world, reaching Number 2 in the US. Andrew was shortlisted for the vacancy, which seemed an achievement in itself, but lost out at the final audition.

Shortly afterwards I'd spotted an advertisement for a rhythm guitarist/backing singer for Peter Jay and the Jaywalkers. Although the highest chart position any of their singles ever reached was 31, the band was very well known. Indeed, I had grown up listening to them singing the hits of other artists on our Bakelite radio. They had also once supported the Beatles on tour and had appeared on *Ready, Steady, Go!*

The band were still performing on the Light Programme lunchtime shows. Not only was the 'needle time' agreement still in force, but the BBC retained its British broadcasting monopoly: it was still take your pick between Light, Home and Third. There weren't even any local BBC stations, which would have at least allowed the Corporation to compete with itself.

I applied for the job with the Jaywalkers. I was still only sixteen, but artists such as Stevie Winwood and Peter Frampton had achieved rock success in their early teens and I saw no reason why I couldn't do the same. I felt I had the pretty-boy looks of Frampton, I could write songs and, while I acknowledged to myself that I'd never be a lead guitarist or lead singer, I knew my chords and had enough of a voice to harmonise sweetly.

I was delighted to be invited to audition. So it was that one windy day, my Höfner Verithin and I headed off from Latimer Road station to a rehearsal space in a nightclub near Leicester Square. I was wearing a thin, light, double-breasted cotton jacket with wide lapels and a faint black stripe, teamed with tight black trousers and Chelsea boots. The soft blue shirt that completed my ensemble had cost me a week's wages. I was convinced I looked the part.

I walked into a room furnished with tiered red velvet seats but no stage. The existing Jaywalkers were ready with all their equipment on a flat, dimly lit bit of the floor. I expected to find myself in a queue of other hopefuls but, to my surprise, I was immediately ushered on to the set.

Peter Jay himself had vacated the drumkit, from where he usually led the band. His place was taken by another drummer so that he could sit four or five rows back in the red velvet seats with an entourage of men in suits. All I had to do was plug my guitar into the equipment provided and take lead vocal and rhythm guitar on the Beatles song 'This Boy'.

The song was the 'B' side of 'I Wanna Hold Your Hand'. I'd never played it before. It wasn't on the Area's playlist. Neither were any other Beatles songs, for that matter. They seemed too sacred to imitate and the rest of the band were more into the Stones. But I knew the track well enough.

'This Boy' has a lovely, mellow, melodic three-part harmony. The lead vocal only really becomes a lead on the rasping middle eight, where it departs from the two harmonising accompanists. Like many early Beatles songs, its apparent simplicity is deceptive. The chords were set out on the sheet music on a stand in front of me and I immediately spotted a tricky D major seventh chord I'd rarely encountered before.

The audition was set up to replicate how the band had to work, often with little rehearsal time before going on air. We played the song straight through twice and then did the middle eight once on its own, at Peter's request.

I was confident I'd done enough to get the job and Peter Jay seemed pleased as he chatted to me amicably afterwards, even mentioning that I'd need to join the Musicians' Union if I was recruited.

I thought my days of shelf-stacking were over. The band's manager had my address, and the phone number of Anthony Jackson's, and every day I expected a letter or a call. But none came.

I wasn't destined to join the band. But as things turned out, it was probably for the best, because the writing was finally on the wall for the band's main source of income, those lunchtime BBC music programmes. Perhaps Peter Jay had seen it, as they broke up not long after my audition. In the late 1970s, he diversified into another branch of the entertainment industry: he bought Great Yarmouth Hippodrome, where Max Miller and Houdini once performed, and Lloyd George held political rallies. Peter Jay is still staging concerts, water spectaculars and circus acts there today, no doubt regretting his failure to make me a Jaywalker.

~

I'm not sure if anyone in North Kensington realised they were living through the Summer of Love. The media reported hippy happenings around the Haight-Ashbury district of San Francisco, and Scott McKenzie's dirge about going there and meeting some gentle people was Number 1 in the UK in September 1967, but I never saw anybody wearing flowers in their hair round our way.

Another slice of Bohemian nonsense dominated the charts that summer. Procol Harum's 'Whiter Shade of Pale' went on and on, literally as well as metaphorically. The band came from Southend and the lyrics reeked of pot. Not that I had any experience of marijuana. I smoked Kensitas (or Du Maurier, if there was a girl to impress). But I knew a good lyric when I heard one, and Procol Harum's 'light fandango' left me cold.

Pink Floyd had headlined the 14-Hour Technicolor Dream Concert at the Ally Pally in north London in the spring, and bands like Soft Machine, Traffic and the Crazy World of Arthur Brown were busy being psychedelic, but the musical event of the year, nationally and internationally, was the release of *Sergeant Pepper's Lonely Hearts Club Band*, which out-psyched them all.

Part of the joy and excitement of following the Beatles in real time lay in the anticipation of each new album. The band's rhapsodic phase had begun with *Rubber Soul*. Its successor, *Revolver*, bore the first fruit of their decision to abandon the stage for the studio. *Sergeant Pepper* saw this phase reach its zenith.

There had been a tantalising taste of what we might expect with the release of 'Strawberry Fields Forever' as a single in February during what I suppose could be described as the Winter of Love. From its opening descending chords, played on a Mellotron, to its closing train-like codicil, this hallucinogenic exploration of Lennon's childhood was extraordinary.

If 'Love Me Do' was the amoeba of the Beatles' canon, 'Strawberry Fields' represented its advanced civilisation. Resonating with the sounds of instruments we'd never heard of, complex key changes and bursts of cello and brass over a foundation of contrasting rhythms, the single was supposedly the result of fifty-five hours in the studio, released at about the time that the Area had been rushing through our sixty minutes at Regent Sound.

'Strawberry Fields' certainly wouldn't have appeared on our

playlist. It was far too complex to be reproduced on stage by them, let alone us, although we did have a crack at the 'B' side, 'Penny Lane', which didn't survive rehearsals.

I wasn't alone in wondering if 'Strawberry Fields' would appear on their eagerly awaited next album, but it didn't. The band stuck to their principle that, with few exceptions, when their fans shelled out good money for a Beatles record, they would be acquiring new music rather than songs they'd already bought as singles. So 'Strawberry Fields Forever' proved to be an hors-d'oeuvre to the main course.

By the time *Sergeant Pepper* was released in June the Beatles had already begun to dismantle the barriers of snobbery and elitism that had previously denied pop music any critical acclaim. The Pulitzer Prize-winning composer Ned Rorem declared that 'She's Leaving Home' was equal to anything Schubert ever wrote; Leonard Bernstein compared their work with Schumann's and the music critic William Mann described Lennon and McCartney as 'outstanding composers', praising their pandiatonic clusters and Aeolian cadences.

Now the music critic of *The Times*, no less, reviewed *Sergeant Pepper* as if it were a classical work. For me and millions of others, it was a classic, if not classical. It was wonderful that the Beatles were being appreciated by a wider, older audience; by those who talked of symphonies and opuses and pandiatonic clusters. But they came from the same background as we did, they had grown with us through the sixties, had astounded us, inspired us, enchanted us. The Beatles belonged to us, not them.

~

Between my audition for Peter Jay and the Jaywalkers and the Grand Theft of the Area's equipment there was a momentous occasion in the history of popular music that sounded the death knell for the pirate radio stations. The British government finally closed the loophole that allowed them to broadcast from international waters and forced them off the air.

Their huge audience was, as far as anyone was able to analyse it, a new demographic of mainly young people who weren't interested in what the BBC had to offer. A response from the BBC was long overdue. The new Marine Offences Act and negotiated adjustments to the 'needle time' agreement with the Musicians' Union allowed them to completely overhaul their service. Three radio stations became four, with the old Light Programme splitting into two, Radio 1 for the kids and Radio 2 for their mums and dads. The generation gap in music really was that stark in the late sixties.

Rock 'n' roll was still so young that it had few adherents over the age of twenty-five. There was no such thing as an ageing rocker in 1967. This musical divide spawned the inter-generational tension that pervaded the sixties and was reflected in its songs. The Rolling Stones sang about what a drag it was to get old while the Who hoped they'd die before they did. I suspect that 'Mother's Little Helper', the Stones' song that paints such a bleak picture of ageing, may have vanished from their playlist now that Mick Jagger is well into his seventies.

In August 1967 I mourned the passing of Radio London, which had been constantly on in the background at Anthony Jackson's supermarket. The station perished magnificently, going off-air to the Beatles' 'Day in the Life', which had been banned by the Beeb because of its supposed references to LSD (dear old 'Auntie' failed to detect any such reference on 'Lucy in the Sky with Diamonds' from the same *Sergeant Pepper* LP). Radio London staff arriving back at Liverpool Street station from Harwich were greeted like returning heroes by crowds of young supporters.

I made sure I was present and correct for the launch of Radio 1 at 7am on the morning of Saturday, 30 September 1967. I rose at 6.30 to an unusually quiet kitchen at Lancaster Road. Today none of the Coxes had to be up for work or school, whereas it was a normal working day for us supermarket workers. On weekdays this was a place of noise and bustle as Mr Cox cooked breakfast. I'd never tasted fried tomatoes before living with the Coxes. Albert cultivated them in large quantities on his allotment and, as the breakfast chef, served them up daily with bacon, toast and the occasional egg. The bowl of cornflakes in front of me now was a poor substitute, but I was glad to have the place to myself as the sacred hour approached. I checked that the Coxes' radio was tuned to 247 metres on the medium wave and waited.

There was a Radio 1 theme tune to be endured before the magic moment when Tony Blackburn – like most of the new station's DJs a former 'pirate' (they were the only ones with the experience) – uttered the first words to be heard on the Beeb's revolutionary new flagship radio station. As 'Flowers in the Rain' by the Move faded and Tony Blackburn reeled off his silly jokes ('Would all motorists taking the M1 to Birmingham kindly bring it back'), I felt the joy of abundance. Having been musically malnourished all my life, forced to scavenge for my daily bread, I was now to have a feast laid on for me every day. Pop music would be as available on the BBC as classical music had always been, free of charge and with no advertising breaks.

The BBC disc jockeys assumed a new prestige, often being considered as cool as the music they played. Some of the old stagers survived – Jimmy Young, for instance, and Pete Murray – but it was the young ones who achieved the cult status. I suppose it was these DJs who seemed to their listeners to be the providers of wall-to-wall pop music rather than a fusty public corporation. My particular favourites were Tony Blackburn, Dave Cash, Kenny Everett and the transatlantic tones of Emperor Rosko.

Radio 1 was not universally popular with its target audience. Some complained that it did not cater adequately for the market the pirates had created, as had been promised; others that it was just another 'establishment' institution. But to me it felt like a monumental advance for young people; as if the state had been forced to acknowledge our existence. Still, more than fifty years on, I think of that day as one of the milestones in my life.

During our bleak coffee shop deliberations after the theft, I tried to impress upon Andrew the likelihood that, with pop music so ubiquitous following the launch of Radio 1, there would be more bands and greater demand for fabulous, good-looking musicians like us. Soon after that conversation Andrew met Ann, a relative of the Coxes, who would be the love of his life. Playing the drums suddenly ceased to be his first priority.

～

The enforced break-up of the Area more or less coincided with the end of my time with the Coxes. Pat and Albert had at long last reached the top of the council waiting list and had been offered a house on a leafy Roehampton estate in south-west London. It was the turn of the building in Lancaster Road in which they had made the happiest of homes for twenty years to face the wrecking ball that had already demolished the slums of Southam Street, along with much of the area, to make way for the Westway, the elevated section of the A40, which was to lift the traffic going in and out of London up and over North Kensington. Some of the replacement housing to be completed in the next decade would stretch skywards. While Southam Street made way for the Trellick Tower, our end of Lancaster Road would be supplanted by a twenty-four-storey block of flats called Grenfell Tower.

My sojourn at 318 Lancaster Road had always been a temporary arrangement and I was grateful to the Coxes for welcoming me into their already overcrowded accommodation for as long as they did. A few months past my seventeenth birthday, I started looking for somewhere else to live. I was not earning very much as a supermarket shelf-stacker and budding pop sensation but a trawl of local papers soon produced a room in the spacious flat of Mrs Kenny, an Irish widow who lived with her grown-up son in Hamlet Gardens, off King Street in Hammersmith, close to where I'd worked for Tesco.

I had to come up with a month's rent in advance. My sister, by now raising her first child, forwarded a loan – not before making another attempt to lure me to Watford, but I was, if anything, even more determined to stay in London, the only place to be if you were waiting for the opportunity to join another band.

I didn't have long to wait. A band called the In-Betweens were looking for a guitarist and Danny had pointed them in my direction. This was a much more professional outfit than the Area. It was managed by an Asian businessman, Arif Ali, and was multi-racial, highly unusual in 1967. Sham Hassan, the bass guitarist, was from Jamaica, 'Mike' Bakridon, the drummer, was Indian, the lead guitarist was Indo-Italian and there was a Guyanese guy on electric organ, who was sometimes available and sometimes not.

The In-Betweens were also highly unusual for having a female lead singer, the stunning Carmen, who was undoubtedly their greatest asset.

It wasn't unknown for a woman to be in a pop group, but it was rare. The Honeycombs, one-hit wonders with 'Have I the Right?' in 1964, had a female drummer, Honey Lantree, and Megan Davies played bass in the Birmingham band the Applejacks, who'd had a huge success the same year with 'Tell Me When'. But these were the exceptions that proved the rule. There were, of course, plenty of female solo singers (Cilla, Dusty, Sandie et al), but women fronting bands, even on the amateur circuit, were few and far between.

Carmen's mother was Indian and her father German. She was nineteen, with long legs emphasised by a very short skirt, and from the moment I saw her I was captivated. I would have joined the band just to be near her. With or without Carmen, this was a great opportunity. As Arif Ali had invested money in the band's equipment, the fact that I had a guitar with no amplifier wasn't a problem. I happily plugged my Höfner into the Marshall amp provided and hitched my star to this wonderful melting pot of a group without even being asked to audition.

The In-Betweens were a band with soul pretensions, although neither Carmen's voice nor mine, as backing vocalist and occasional lead, sounded that soulful. Having said that, as a smoker and frequent sufferer of coughs and colds, I thought my voice bore a faint resemblance to Wilson Pickett's when it was croaking out of a sore throat.

In fact Pickett's 'Midnight Hour' was on our playlist (but only when the organist turned up), together with some more obscure rhythm and blues stuff, which I had to learn, and pop songs like Cat Stevens' 'The First Cut Is the Deepest', a hit that year for P. P. Arnold, and the Bee Gees' 'To Love Somebody'. I had three solo numbers where I took centre stage, fulfilling my overwhelming desire to show off.

I'd sung 'All or Nothing' with the Area, all knees together and fringe flopping, à la Stevie Marriott, as I tore into the climax, 'For me, for me, FOR ME,' even throwing in the odd 'keep on keeping on' and 'let me tell you, children'. The second one was 'Ticket to Ride', admittedly inspired more by the Vanilla Fudge version, which was slower and more soulful, than the Beatles original.

My *pièce de résistance* – and, though I say it myself, one of the highlights of our set – was The Troggs' 'Wild Thing'. For this I stood mid-stage with Carmen not just dancing round me but, in the slow bits ('I wanna know for sure . . .'), actually entwined round me, an elegant, short-skirted thigh across my legs, perfumed arms around my neck, beautiful, soft brown eyes staring into mine, hot breath on my cheek.

Carmen and I were born to duet on that song, destined to be together in the centre of that stage. It should have forged the deepest, most volcanic passion since Cathy met Heathcliff. There was only one problem. Carmen was totally and absolutely

Above: My mother Lily (*second from right*) and father Steve next to her at the wedding of one of her sisters, Auntie Jean (*third from left*), to Uncle George (*in uniform*) in 1946.

Left: Linda and me dancing.

Below: My teachers at Bevington Primary School. Miss Woofenden, who taught us music, is second from the right, next to the slightly detached headmaster, Mr Gemmill.

Lonnie Donegan in full skiffle mode in front of a rather more intimate audience than when I saw him at the Chiswick Empire.

Me and Colin James. As can be seen, I had a penchant for matelot shirts and we both favoured the folded-arms stance. While it wasn't posed that way, the black-and-white image just happens to have a photo of the Stones and a Beatles album cover in the background.

Left: Chuck Berry doing the duck walk he performed when I saw him at the Hammersmith Odeon in 1964.

Right: Dereck Tapper, a child of the Windrush generation, was with me at infant, primary and grammar school. This 1970 press photo records his appearance in what was then the startling innovation of a mixed-race production of *Romeo and Juliet* at a teacher-training college in Exeter.

Left: Bert Weedon's *Play in a Day* instruction manual, which should have been prosecuted under the Trade Descriptions Act.

Below: Denmark Street – aka Tin Pan Alley – with Margo and the Marvettes, perhaps on their way to record at Regent Sound, where the Area made its demo disc.

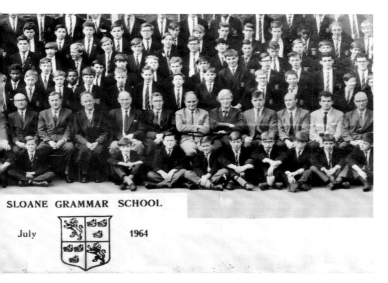

SLOANE GRAMMAR SCHOOL

July 1964

The Sloane School photo with (*far right to left, sitting on the ground*) John Williams, Andrew Wiltshire and me trying to look cool and disinterested. Dereck Tapper is five rows directly behind me with eyes averted from the camera. Mr Carlen is the first teacher seated on the left with hands on knees, and my other favourite, Mr Pallai, is six places to the right of him, in the light suit.

Anthony Jackson's in East Sheen, at around the time I worked there in the sixties. It has since been replaced by Johnson's Shoes.

Above: One of the cards that Danny had printed for our 'beat group'.

Right: My Höfner Verithin guitar, with Venetian double cutaways, mother-of-pearl inlay on the head and neck, black scratchboard and Bigsby tremolo unit.

The Beatles: the Fab Four played 'All You Need Is Love' in front of a global television audience of 400 million in 1967.

Left: Judy and me on our wedding day, posing in front of somebody else's beribboned car.

Right: Celebrating our wedding at a Hammersmith pub. *From left to right*: me, Judy, Andrew, Albert Cox, Ann and Carole Cox. My sister was the photographer.

Below: A family jam session in the seventies. *Left to right*: Jamie, Natalie, me and Emma. Note the painted white walls of our Britwell home and my Eko twelve-string guitar.

Above: David Bowie's facial lightning flash on the cover of *Aladdin Sane* was quickly copied by his fans.

Left: Kate Bush: a brilliant artist who could never be accused of being too prolific.

Below: Elvis Costello: the artist I've seen perform everywhere from the London Palladium to Sands Leisure Centre in Carlisle.

Below: This is not a new supergroup, just the line-up for an edition of *The Andrew Marr Show* in May 2014, hosted by Nick Robinson and featuring me (and my Höfner guitar), Theresa May (when she was home secretary) and the band Noah and the Whale.

uninterested in me. She was completely immune to what I was convinced was a magnetic and irresistible charm. As I found out soon enough, she had already fallen for Mike Bakridon. The bloody drummer. In all the annals of pop history, girls have never fallen for the guy on the drums. But Carmen broke the mould in more ways than one, and she and Mike went on to spend the rest of their lives together.

Wild thing, indeed.

~

Boxing Day 1967. I'm at Linda's for Christmas. Tonight we'll watch the film the Beatles have made for TV, *Magical Mystery Tour*. It contains six new songs, which have been available since before Christmas on an EP for under a pound.

From 'Strawberry Fields' in February, through the release of the *Sergeant Pepper* album and the single 'All You Need Is Love', it has been an incredible year for Beatles fans. I saw their debut performance of 'All You Need Is Love' on 25 June, sitting in the Coxes' lounge with Mr and Mrs Cox, Danny and Carole, Tony and Paul – the seven of us strewn across settees, armchairs and the floor awaiting what had been billed as the 'greatest event in television history'.

We were part of an estimated global audience of between 400 and 700 million to witness the first live international satellite television production, *Our World*, in which artists representing nineteen different countries contributed to a huge shared experience lasting over two hours. Those participating included Maria Callas, the Vienna Boys Choir, Pablo Picasso and Marshall McLuhan, the Canadian master of media theory responsible for the concept that 'the medium is the message'.

I'd had to wait until the very end for Britain's contribution, when the cameras took us live to the Abbey Road studios, where the Fab Four were recording their new single as the world looked on. John, Paul, George and Ringo, accompanied by an orchestra, were perched on high stools above a gathering of guests, many of them sitting cross-legged on the parquet floor like infant schoolchildren at morning assembly, looking up at the Beatles as if to pay homage to the undisputed masters of their musical genre. It included such rock luminaries as Mick Jagger, Eric Clapton and Graham Nash.

Now they are rounding off a triumphant year with a new three minutes of pure, uncomplicated pop. 'Hello, Goodbye' is the Christmas Number 1 and *Magical Mystery Tour* is being offered to TV viewers as the highlight of the festive programming.

I am settled in with Linda and Mike in their snug front room in Watford. Six-month-old Renay is asleep upstairs. We crack a few walnuts while waiting for we know not what. There have been no previews beyond the music. Unfortunately, those six tracks are the best thing about the Beatles' film. The improvised comedy drama is self-indulgent rubbish and will be rightly panned by the critics, two of whom are sitting beside me. Linda and Mike have never been huge Beatles fans, but we all expected better than this.

Still, I am not too disappointed. It has been a glorious year for their music, and that is what the Beatles are about. I seek solace in a sandwich, concluding that I'd rather eat a turkey than watch one.

On 30 December, I was back at Linda's again for her New

Year's Eve party, held that year, like most people's celebrations, on the Saturday night. There was no New Year's Day bank holiday then so it gave everyone the Sunday to get their breath back before work on Monday.

It had been touch and go whether I would make it. The In-Betweens were playing at our home venue, a pub called the Pied Bull in Islington where we stored our gear and performed in front of our most devoted fans. The landlord had booked us well in advance for his busiest night of the festive season and it was a commitment we couldn't break. Not that I wanted to. I had only agreed to go to Watford so as not to upset my sister.

The In-Betweens were on top form that night, with my 'Ticket to Ride' going down a storm. We came offstage at 11pm and I managed to get to Linda's house by about half-past midnight, catching the last train from Euston to Watford. The front room, back room and kitchen were packed with people I didn't know: neighbours, friends and assorted waifs and strays. Linda whispered something to me concerning a girl named Cox, but I couldn't hear her properly above all the merriment and thought she was talking about one of Pat and Albert's family.

Linda was in fact pointing out her friend Judy Cox, with whom she'd done her nursery nurse training at Brixton College, and reminding me that I'd met her once when a gang of Linda's friends had come to Pitt House. Judy was dark and attractive with a Cilla Black hairstyle and a dazzling smile. That night she and I stayed up talking after the other guests had left and my sister and brother-in-law had gone to bed. We sat in Linda's back room, with the radio turned down low so as not to disturb the two little girls who slept upstairs: Renay, my baby niece, and Natalie, Judy's fourteen-month-old daughter.

On the final day of a golden year that overflowed with unforgettable music – and one which included the thrill of having my own reproduced on vinyl – the record played most regularly through those wee small hours was 'Nights in White Satin' by the Moody Blues. If I close my eyes I can hear it now as I drift back to that house in Watford, where my younger self was smoking, drinking, talking and falling in love with Judy, the woman who was to become my wife.

1968

Hey, Jude

COMMUNICATING WITH ONE'S inamorata was no easier for my generation in 1968 than it would have been when my father was walking out with my mother a quarter of a century previously. There was no phone at Mrs Kenny's, nor was there one in the house Judy shared with her grandmother at 3 Camelford Road, London W11. I got the address from Linda, and wrote to Judy to ask her for a date. I filled four sides of thin blue notepaper telling her how much I'd enjoyed our evening together in Watford and how much I hoped she would agree to see me again.

My head spun with giddy delight when she replied, taking only a side and a half to accept my invitation. Now all I had to do was write again with a date, time and place. I paid 2d extra postage, just to be on the safe side, to suggest that we met at the barriers in Hammersmith Broadway underground station at 7.30pm on Monday, 8 January. Having considered the matter carefully, I'd settled on this as a mutually convenient rendez-vous point. Judy would have only a short walk to Ladbroke

Grove station and four stops on the Metropolitan Line; I could either walk all the way there from my end of King Street or just hop on one of the many buses that ran along this major thoroughfare to the Broadway.

Next there was the thorny question of where to take her. In fact it wasn't all that thorny, seeing as my limited resources wouldn't stretch to anything more luxurious than the pictures. Protocol demanded that the privilege of paying must always fall to the male of the species. The concept of 'going Dutch' may have gained some traction among university students but working-class culture dictated that however 'boracic' a man might be, to ask his girlfriend to contribute would be to abandon all claim to masculinity. I checked what was showing at the three cinemas in Hammersmith so that I would be able to demonstrate my gallantry by at least offering my date a meaningful choice.

The big day dawned cold and damp, the weather contrasting with my emotions as I counted down the hours, longing for the evening to arrive. I dressed carefully while listening to the blue transistor radio my manager at Anthony Jackson's allowed me to bring home with me every evening so that I had some entertainment in my bedsit. I donned a white Ben Sherman button-down shirt, black trousers and my favourite hound's-tooth jacket, which I'd picked up second hand. As it was cold I added my sister's old Brixton College scarf, which had somehow ended up in my possession, throwing it carelessly round my neck as a final flourish.

At 6.30pm I set off on the twenty-minute walk to Hammersmith station, telling myself that it was best to be early just in case Judy was as well. I got there before seven and stood to attention, watching the passengers disgorge from train after train. Hammersmith is at the end of the Metropolitan Line, so everyone had to get off, and as there was only one exit it was impossible for me to miss anybody alighting from those cherry-red carriages.

I waited until 7.50 before giving up and going home, crushed by disappointment. Back at Hamlet Gardens I began to panic. Could I have written 8.30pm in the letter by mistake? So I went back, this time on a 73 bus, and stood forlornly at the station entrance for another hour before trailing back to my bedsit, where I wrote a self-pitying song entitled 'Approaching 7.30', seeking solace, as ever, in music.

~

Judy never received my letter. Perhaps I addressed it wrongly, perhaps it got trapped at the bottom of a mail sack, or maybe her dog, Suzie, ate it fresh off the doormat. Who knows? All I do know is how easily a letter undelivered could lead to a romance unrequited. Indeed, life and literature are full of stories where it has.

When I turned on the radio the morning after our abortive date, Glen Campbell was singing 'By the Time I Get to Phoenix'. I'd never heard of the singer or the song, or the man who wrote it – and so many classics familiar to us all – Jimmy Webb, but its mournful beauty matched my mood perfectly. By the time I got to East Sheen (which did not have quite the same ring to it), I'd resolved to find out whether Judith Elizabeth Cox was a lost cause. I used the phone at work to call Linda for the number of Brook Green nursery, where she had worked with Judy before moving to Watford. Then, on my lunch break, I walked to the phone box on the corner where I could have a more private conversation with the woman I thought had stood me up.

It was then that I learned the truth. My spirits soared as I realised I hadn't been rejected. A queue formed outside the kiosk, as they tended to do at lunchtime, but everyone else would have to wait. I had arrangements to make, and this time I needed to be sure they had been safely communicated.

Judy told me that in two days' time, on 11 January, it would be her twenty-first birthday. She agreed to celebrate the occasion by going with me to see the film *Here We Go Round the Mulberry Bush*.

This time everything went smoothly. The film was one of those whimsical 'coming of age' British comedies popular in the sixties, all randy blokes and leggy blondes. The young hero worked in a supermarket and was trying to forge a relationship with an older woman. The parallels were not lost on me, a supermarket worker, celebrating Judy's coming of age with my own still four years away.

The best thing about the film was the title song, recorded by Stevie Winwood's new 'supergroup', Traffic. It blared out over the titles as we rushed for the exit along with the entire audience, to avoid having to stand motionless for the national anthem. 'Come on, let's get out before the Queen' was an injunction common to cinemagoers throughout the land in those days, and would prompt a minor stampede. 'God Save the Queen' was played as soon as the credits ended and the drum roll preceding the anthem created a scene like something from a science-fiction novel as the stragglers who hadn't made it out in time were forced to freeze, zombie-like, mid-stride, to show their respect.

Poor Judy. A twenty-first birthday was a big thing. Twenty-one was still the 'age of majority', when adulthood was conferred on you, along with the right to vote. It would be lowered to eighteen in 1970, but even for some time after that, turning twenty-one was a cause for celebration, its status as a milestone being so culturally established.

Young girls in particular had parties and special meals and presents. Judy had nobody to organise a big family do for her, having lost her mother, who had died in childbirth, along with the baby, when Judy was a year old. Her father had immediately abandoned his kids and run off with his girlfriend. Judy had eventually been taken in by her maternal grandparents while her two older brothers went to Dr Barnardo's. Now it was just Judy, her grandmother and her baby daughter Natalie, Judy's grandfather having died over a decade earlier.

Judy's Italian student fiancé, Natalie's father, had fled back to Italy when he discovered Judy was pregnant three years into their relationship. She had been determined to keep the baby, come what may, and had developed the thick skin and defiant demeanour that was a necessary part of the armour of the sixties single mother.

So all Judy got for her twenty-first birthday was a night at the pictures and the box of Cadbury's Milk Tray I'd purchased hurriedly in a newsagent's on my way to meet her. She placed this in her handbag as I accompanied her home to Camelford Road. We parted with a brief kiss on the doorstep as her fearsome nan twitched the curtains at a window in the upstairs rooms she and Judy occupied.

Upon these unpromising foundations a romantic relationship was built. Now my free time was divided between Judy (or Jude, as I was soon calling her) and the In-Betweens. She came with me to some of our gigs but she was reluctant to lumber her grandmother with too many babysitting duties. By Valentine's Day I was quoting the latest Bee Gees song on my (anonymous) card: 'It's only words, and words are all I have . . .' And by the spring we were engaged, with a wedding date set for July.

Between our engagement and our wedding, disaster struck for the In-Betweens. In a repeat of the catastrophe that had put paid to the Area, thieves broke into the Pied Bull and stole all of our equipment from the room above the bar where it was stored. This time my beloved Höfner Verithin went as well.

Everything had been going so well for the band. A noted A&R man (artists and repertoire – basically a talent scout) was interested in us, as was Pat Meehan from EMI, whose attendance at one of our gigs had led to an audition for a recording contract at a studio in Shepherd's Bush. Now it was déjà vu all over again.

Immediately after the theft I went across to Islington to see Sham, the Jamaican bass guitarist, my closest friend in the band, who was a postman (higher grade) at the Northern District Office of Royal Mail in Upper Street, directly opposite the Pied Bull. Sham took me to the canteen and, over a coffee, railed against the landlord of the pub, whom he accused of lax security and even suspected of complicity in the robbery. He was keen for the two of us to form a new band together, and he thought Arif Ali might give us some financial help to do it. His idea was for a group loosely based on the Equals, a band that was about to hit the big time with 'Baby, Come Back', which would be Number 1 by July.

I told him I couldn't afford to continue my quest for rock stardom. Getting to gigs and rehearsals was a logistical nightmare. I was finding it increasingly difficult to trek from Hammersmith to the Siberian wilds of Islington to practise, and although there was an In-Betweens van, since the rest of the band lived in north London I usually had to make my own way to the venues. But what really changed everything was that I'd plighted my troth to Judy who, in March, had told me she was pregnant with our child. By Christmas I was going to be a married man with two children.

My priority now had to be to find a proper job that paid me more than Anthony Jackson's. There was another problem looming at the supermarket where I'd worked perfectly happily for the past year: it was soon to be taken over by Tesco. If I didn't leave before long, I'd find myself back working for the company I'd deserted – and they might not be too delighted to have my name on their payroll.

When I explained all this to Sham, my friend came up with a much more sensible suggestion: I should become a postman.

'Let me tell you sumtin',' he said in his broad Caribbean accent, pulling his chair closer to mine. 'Post Office pay is crap. The *rasclats* that run it can't get any staff, you understand me? So as a result dere is as much overtime as you want – first six hours, time and a quarter; second six hours, time and a half, every ting from thirteenth hour onward, *double bubble*!' Sham collapsed into a giggling heap. 'I swear dere are guys in here who live in de place and probably earn more than de postmaster general.'

Sham wiped the tears from his eyes as he reflected on the hilarity of the situation. His was an effective if unconventional recruitment drive. As we walked back to the office gates I observed the warmth and comradeship of these blue-uniformed civil servants towards one another. I had a sense that it would be a good place to work.

So I decided there and then that, while I couldn't follow Sham in his musical pursuits, I would try to follow him into the Post Office.

I'd take up music again at some stage, obviously. I was still destined to be a rock 'n' roll star. Just not yet.

~

There was no music at our wedding at Hammersmith Register Office on 27 July 1968. I don't remember if it was even the done thing at civil ceremonies, which were pretty basic and businesslike then – I left all the details to Judy – but in the days of record-players and reel-to-reel tape-recorders it wouldn't have been very easy to organise even if it was permitted. Andrew was my best man and the bride travelled to her wedding by tube with her nan and Natalie – three generations of women with a genealogical gap where Judy's mother should have been. My sister took some photographs before we all repaired to a pub by the Thames for a lunchtime drink.

Having gone home for the afternoon, my wife and I were back in Hammersmith that evening to celebrate with a meal out with Andrew and Ann. This in itself was a novelty. The closest I ever got to a restaurant were my visits to a cafeteria in my lunch breaks at Remington's to make use of the 3s (15p) daily luncheon vouchers issued as part of my wages.

On the evening of my wedding I ordered a mushroom omelette. It was the only thing on the menu I was sure about, there being no steak pie and chips.

I returned once again to North Kensington to live with Judy at her nan's house in Camelford Road, which snaked between Ladbroke Grove and St Marks Road. The four of us, Judy, Nan, Natalie and me, plus Suzie the dog, occupied the top two floors of yet another condemned house. Andrew's girlfriend Ann took over my room at Mrs Kenny's, having decided to move to London from her home town of Aylesbury to be closer to Andrew. They were married the following year.

I was now working for the Post Office, not in North Kensington, or at Sham's comradely workplace in Islington, but in Barnes, London SW13, the leafy, upmarket area through which I'd passed on the bus every day from Hammersmith to Anthony Jackson's in East Sheen. I'd liked the look of Barnes.

A few months later, Andrew decided he'd had enough of butchering and followed me into the GPO. His parents had paid for him to have driving lessons for his eighteenth birthday the previous December. He passed his test first time and came to our little sorting office on Barnes Green as a postman/driver.

To get to work by my starting time of 5.30am I cycled the four miles from Ladbroke Grove to Barnes, relishing the empty streets going in and dodging the heavy traffic coming back. All of my thirty or so new workmates were men. Most of them were much older than me and a majority had fought in the Second World War – a generation who were now into their forties or fifties. At Barnes they appreciated the military overtones of Post Office life and wore their blue serge uniforms with pride.

My ex-forces workmates didn't talk to me about what they'd done in the war, let alone boast about it. I would hear them chatting to one another and pieced together their individual military histories from fragments of conversation. Billy Fairs, the union rep, had helped liberate Italy and returned home to Mortlake with an Italian bride. They lived the rest of their lives together in a council flat by the Thames. Les Griffiths had served in the Fleet Air Arm; Frank Dainton had been a Guardsman – tall and straight-backed, he always wore the full Post Office uniform, including waistcoat, collar and tie, no matter how warm the weather. Peter Simonelli had been in Greece and, like Billy, had married a girl he'd met on active service.

In the sorting office, where we prepared for our 'walks', the radio was not allowed. The only music came from the men themselves. Les would occasionally burst into 'If You Were the Only Girl in the World' and Freddie Binks, a tall bachelor who thought he was God's gift to women, would entertain us with his selection from *West Side Story*. Repetition of his version of 'Maria' ('I've just met a man named Maria') didn't seem to diminish his conviction this was the funniest line anyone had ever heard.

And every morning at about 10.30 when we'd sorted up the 'Irish' (as the second delivery was known as in London), 'Nobby' Clarke would remove the pipe that resided almost permanently in his mouth (though in accordance with Post Office rules, it remained unlit in the office) to serenade us with a medley of songs by his favourite singer, Al Bowlly.

His performance was met with the same catcalls and good-natured abuse every single day. 'Nobby' could take it. I'd wrongly deduced he'd been at Dunkirk until Billy Fairs put me right. In fact he had been in a Japanese prisoner of war camp for four years. There was nothing we could do to stop Nobby singing and no abuse imaginable that could match what he'd gone through as a young man.

It was at home one Saturday morning when, unusually, I had a day off, that I first heard 'Hey, Jude'. I thought it was sublime, from its introduction-free beginning to its singalong end. With a new wife named Judy, it had an extra resonance for me and, as a proper homage to her, Paul's tribute to 'Jude' was certainly a vast improvement on 'Judy in Disguise (With Glasses)', which had been a hit for John Fred and His Playboy Band when Judy and I had first got together. Discovering later that McCartney had actually written the song for John's young son Julian and tweaked the name did nothing to weaken the connection for me. And the fact that the name in the song was 'Jude', as opposed to 'Judy', even strengthened it. The further abbreviation suggested greater intimacy, like the French distinction between *tu* and *vous*.

Obviously I had to buy that record, straitened though our circumstances were. Our joint aversion to hire purchase forced us to save for the washing machine, vacuum cleaner and fridge we didn't have, and spare cash was non-existent. I decided to return to the record shop in Portobello Road where Linda and I had bought the first 45s we ever owned eight years before. I saw it as symbolic of my rapid maturity from snotty-nosed kid to married man; from 'Fings Ain't What They Used T'Be' to 'Hey, Jude'.

At work, there was only one other Beatles fan, a young post-man called Brian Green. Apart from Andrew, Brian was the only other colleague of roughly my age, having joined the Post Office as a telegram boy straight from school. As he was also a QPR supporter and we had a similar sense of humour, we had bonded straight away. Brian and I eulogised what we agreed was one of the Fab Four's finest singles. In November the release of the band's ninth studio album, *The Beatles*, which would become better known as the White Album, gave us thirty new tracks to savour and discuss.

Brian told me that the track 'Rocky Raccoon' had been com-posed collectively by Paul, John and the former Dylan impersonator Donovan, who'd sat around smoking cannabis and taking it in turns to contribute a line to the lyric. I had no idea where Brian got this from, but it rang true and seemed to explain the casual way in which this sprawling album had been created. Brian's story would be confirmed by the reams of books and articles devoted over the years to every detail of the Beatles' lives. The song was written in India during their tran-scendental meditation phase, at a time when they were known to have been joined at their retreat by Donovan.

Brian and I concurred that if our heroes had dispensed with such self-indulgence the White Album could have been a fifteen-track classic.

~

One day, covering a new delivery for a colleague who'd gone sick, I was passing a house on Riverside in Barnes when I noticed a blue plaque fixed to the front wall which announced that this had once been the home of Gustav Holst, composer of *The Planets*. Standing in the murky morning light, my mind went back to Mr Dearlove, my music teacher at Sloane, who'd tried so hard to inculcate an appreciation of classical music in his pupils. I remembered a lesson where he'd played *The Planets* to us, urging the thirty-five boys in his class to silently contemplate the visual images he was confident the music would evoke.

The trouble was, having been told that the piece was about seven planets, I found it impossible to allow the music to create the image, feeling obliged instead to imprint on my mind a picture of Jupiter or Mars or Pluto (the planet that had always fascinated me most, but which had yet to be discovered when Holst wrote his masterpiece). Was it permissible, one boy asked sarcastically, to think of Mercury while listening to Neptune? The lesson deteriorated into near-anarchy and in the end Mr Dearlove gave up. We could be made to behave but what went on in our imaginations was beyond instruction.

Mr Dearlove wasn't a music snob. On another occasion he allowed one of my classmates to bring in a Roy Orbison LP and encouraged us to sing along to 'Blue Bayou'. And his attempt to instil in us a regard for Holst may not have been entirely unsuccessful. In my case it certainly planted a seed, because I came to love *The Planets*, a work of which I would have been unaware had it not been for Mr Dearlove.

I wasn't the only one. Plenty of twentieth-century musicians were inspired by Holst. Themes from *The Planets* were particularly popular among the denizens of prog rock, for some reason, and can be discerned in recordings by King Crimson, Jimmy Page and Yes. And Manfred Mann's Earth Band's 'Joybringer' is an arrangement of 'Jupiter'.

Judy had a black English Electric record-player and a modest collection of LPs. There were a couple by Pete Seeger, a live album by Peter, Paul and Mary, the soundtrack of *West Side Story* and various records by her two favourite French singers, Richard Anthony and Françoise Hardy.

I'd allowed my singles to go with Linda to Watford, retaining my LPs (most of the Beatles' albums, *Pet Sounds*, *Younger Than Yesterday* by the Byrds, Bob Dylan's *Bringing it All Back Home*, *Roger the Engineer* by the Yardbirds, *Aftermath* by the Stones and a couple by Chuck Berry).

I still dreamed of having enough money to buy all the records I wanted. In the meantime Judy made an addition to the collection by buying me the White Album for Christmas. The best gift of all that year, though, was our beautiful daughter Emma, born on Christmas Eve.

1969

Space Oddity

DOWN THE YEARS the songs accumulate, almost all of them destined for a fleeting moment in the sun, fondly remembered by a few, forgotten by most. Some live on, or are reincarnated, as emblematic of a bygone time, remaining for ever trapped in their era; others inspire or influence new music. A few, a very few, become immortal in the form in which they were originally recorded, sounding as fresh to each new generation as they did to their own.

As an avid reader of *Melody Maker* and the *Record Mirror*, I kept myself informed on all emerging new acts, no matter how obscure. So David Bowie had been on my radar for a couple of years. I'd heard some of the tracks from his eponymous first LP and was mildly impressed, although I dismissed his 'Laughing Gnome' single, which sank without trace on its first release, as risible. Its only distinctive feature was a vocal similarity to Anthony Newley.

With the release of 'Space Oddity' in the summer of 1969, all was forgiven and (in the case of 'The Laughing Gnome') forgotten.

With my young family, I had just moved out of North Kensington, for good – and, for the first time in my life, out of London – to the council house we'd been allocated at 234 Long Furlong Drive on the Britwell estate in Slough, twenty miles away in the Buckinghamshire countryside.

Camelford Road was next on the demolition schedule – the entire street was to be wiped off the map in the great Westway advance that had already seen two of my previous addresses disappear. The council were obliged to rehouse all those affected but, having been on their waiting list for less than a year, we had one chance, take it or leave it. The house we were offered was semi-detached with two bedrooms, an indoor toilet, a bath and not just one garden but two, front and back. Judy and I felt as if we'd won the pools. We accepted the offer.

Judy's grandmother, who'd been on the waiting list for years, was entitled to at least three choices. She wanted to remain in London living independently, which was a relief to me, if not to Judy. Nan and I had never got on. She had been close to Judy's Italian fiancé and was understandably baffled as to what her well-educated granddaughter (Judy was a Burlington grammar-school girl who'd gone on to teacher training college before switching to nursery nursing) was doing with a teenage shelf-stacker-turned-postman. Nan moved to a cosy flat in sheltered accommodation on the Cuckoo estate in Hanwell.

The only problem with our move was the timing. It had to take place over the July weekend when the Rolling Stones were giving a free concert in Hyde Park, which Judy and I had been planning to attend.

I was ambivalent about the Stones. Having been excited by their live performances at the Wimbledon Palais before they'd conquered the world, I was less impressed by their records. The media had been keen to manufacture a division between the Stones and the Beatles that remained artificial for most music fans who listened to both. More crudely, the Beatles were portrayed, in their pre-psychedelic phase at least, as ideal son-in-law material and the longer-haired Stones as the kind of unwashed wasters that any decent father would guard his daughters against. When rivalry between the two sets of fans arose, those supporting the Beatles would be quick to point out that not only had the Stones' second single, 'I Wanna Be Your Man', been a Lennon/McCartney composition (they'd gone to Chuck Berry for their first), it was one considered so insignificant that it had been given to Ringo to sing on the Beatles' second album.

While Lennon and McCartney had written hundreds of songs before they were famous, Jagger and Richards had written none, even during the early days of their success. 'It's All Over Now' was an American R&B number and 'Not Fade Away' an old Buddy Holly 'B' side. In fact nothing written by 'Jagger/Richards' emerged until the third Stones album, on which a couple of mediocre tracks were originals.

By their fourth album (my favourite, *Aftermath*), every song was suddenly by Mick and Keith. They'd progressed in a short while from writing nothing to coming up with songs as sophisticated as 'Out of Time' and 'Mother's Little Helper'. The rumour was that Andrew Loog Oldham, the band's manager, had asked his Beatles counterpart, Brian Epstein, if John and Paul could spend a weekend with Mick and Keith to teach them the art of songwriting. This had a ring of truth to it. It was the kind of crash course in songwriting that wouldn't be available at evening classes and would help to explain how Mick and Keith had managed such a steep learning curve.

By July 1969 I had enough appreciation for the Stones to want to be at that Hyde Park concert. It would have taken us only twenty minutes to walk to the park from Camelford Road. And the fact that the event was taking place only two days after Brian Jones drowned in his swimming pool made it a particularly poignant occasion. But while Mick Jagger was reading Shelley and hundreds of white butterflies were being released in tribute to Jones, we were driving off in a small removals van to begin a new life on one of the biggest council estates in Britain.

I had transferred my Post Office employment from Barnes to Slough, and by the Monday morning we were settling in and I was cycling into the sorting office.

It was on the Friday of that same week that 'Space Oddity' was released. Bowie, pre-Ziggy Stardust and Aladdin Sane, had made his first attempt to put the mysteries of outer space to music. Such was the originality of the song and the otherworldliness of its production that the record could itself have been beamed in from another planet. It was certainly in tune with the zeitgeist. Stanley Kubrick's film *2001: A Space Odyssey*, from which Bowie must have taken his inspiration and (with an ironic twist) his song title, had been released the previous year, and the books of writers such as Ray Bradbury, Arthur C. Clarke and Brian Aldiss were surging in popularity.

Clarke collaborated with Kubrick on his film, writing the novel on which it was based – at the same time as the movie was being made, as it turned out. A unique *modus operandi*, not to say a labour-intensive and expensive one. Now viewed as one of the most influential films of all time, it also brought the music of Strauss to a new audience, as well as that of contemporary composers Aram Khachaturian and Györgi Ligeti.

Bowie's record company had picked the release date carefully. Five days later, the Apollo 11 space mission was launched and Bowie's little science-fiction story about Major Tom and his lonely exile in space became intertwined with the giant leap for mankind.

Over half a billion people around the world watched those grainy black-and-white images of Neil Armstrong and Buzz Aldrin walking on the moon, gaping in awe as the event unfolded in real time. Judy and I were among them. For us the sense that we were entering a new era was emphasised by the dramatic change in our own world. Only a fortnight before, we had been living in the slums of west London. Now here we were in our own comfortable home, with the majestic beauty of Burnham Beeches just down the road. We couldn't have been more content. Whereas my mother had died with the council house she'd dreamed of still beyond her grasp, I had been allocated one at just nineteen. (I wasn't even old enough to hold the tenancy: it had to be put in Judy's sole name.)

And now we were privileged to witness something unimaginable when my parents were born: human beings stepping on to another planet. As I saw those two men in their spacesuits cavorting like kids against the backdrop of the earth spinning below, a constant question ran on a loop through my mind to the chords of D7, C and G: 'Can you hear me Major Tom? Can you hear me Major Tom?'

1970

After the Gold Rush

IT WAS TIME to begin decorating at 234 Long Furlong Drive. In preparation for the task at hand I had become a close observer of the décor in the the large houses of Dawes East Road, Pipers Close and Linkswood Road to which I now delivered on my regular mail round in the prosperous little town of Burnham, half a mile from the Britwell.

There were no council houses like ours on my route. Burnham was populated by professionals: accountants, solicitors and bank managers who'd be heading off to work as I was completing the early-morning delivery. By and large their wives stayed at home. I'd exchange pleasantries with them on the second, midday delivery, when those with small children, which was most of them, were around during the hours between taking their offspring to school and picking them up again. Some of the older women had other jobs. I remember one who taught languages at evening classes and another who ran a boutique called Brandy's in Burnham High Street.

On our little patch of the Britwell estate, daily life wasn't dissimilar: the men went off to work while the women stayed at home. There weren't many part-time jobs around that women could combine with child-rearing and my union at the Post Office wasn't alone in trying to keep things that way. The received wisdom was that women only worked 'for pin money' and, as far as organised labour was concerned, full-time jobs were the only ones that mattered. Working-class women took in home work, such as sewing, to earn some extra cash. Judy was soon running a playgroup from which she earned little, if anything. It was handy, though, as she could take our two small children with her.

Meanwhile, I worked every Saturday and most Sundays (which was double time and pensionable – not that I gave even a fleeting thought to retirement in those days). On average I worked about seventy hours a week – more even than Sham, my bass-playing friend, could have envisaged when he convinced me to become a postman.

It left me little time to wield a paintbrush, impatient though we were to decorate our first nesting place and to paint over the lurid orange patterned wallpaper we'd inherited, an acquired taste even for the 1960s.

We decided that I would dedicate my week's winter leave to this purpose. So, in February 1970, Judy and the kids went to stay with Linda and Mike, who were now living in Tring in Hertfordshire, leaving me the space and necessary tranquillity to exercise the talent I was convinced was part of my genetic heritage.

Since my father had been a painter and decorator, I imagined that the required skills would be embedded somewhere in my DNA. It was true that I'd never actually observed my father painting or decorating anything. To be fair, the places where we'd lived all had damp walls and peeling paper on which any attempts to brandish a paintbrush would probably have been futile. In adulthood, I'd only ever lived in other people's houses and so, at nineteen years old, I had yet to prise the lid off a tin of paint, let alone apply the contents smoothly to an appropriate surface.

Our house may have been owned by the council but we thought of it as ours, and indeed our name would be on the rent book for as long as we wanted it to be. This was the foundation of our settled serenity.

I was determined that my first experience of decorating should be a success. The market research I'd conducted on the houses on my delivery revealed that most had plain white walls. This seemed to me to have two advantages. The first was that it gave a bright, fresh feel to the room and the second was that, with enough coats of paint, I could obliterate the awful orange paper without having to replace it. The process of wallpapering frightened the life out of me. The chorus of one of the old cockney songs in my father's wedding reception repertoire, 'When Father Papered the Parlour', echoed in my head.

> When Father papered the parlour
> You couldn't see him for paste,
> Dabbing it here, dabbing it there,
> Paste and paper everywhere.
> Mother was stuck to the ceiling,
> The kids were stuck to the floor,
> You never saw such a blooming family so stuck up before.

At least there would be no danger of my little family ending up like that. They would be safely exiled. Besides, there would be no need for paste and paper as Judy agreed with my suggestion that our 'parlour' be painted white.

There was something else I'd noticed as I peered into the living rooms of my customers. They invariably had their books on display. Mine had been accumulating in an egg box for years. By egg box, I don't mean the cartons containing six or a dozen eggs found on supermarket shelves, I mean the substantial ones, big as coffins, in which the cartons arrived at the supermarket warehouse.

I must have picked mine up from Tesco to transport my books from Battersea to North Kensington when I moved in with the Coxes. By then I'd amassed a substantial number of mostly second-hand volumes from haunts like the Popular Book Shop in the Hammersmith Road, where I'd swapped my collection of *Charles Buchan's Football Monthly* magazines for a stack of murder mysteries by writers such as Agatha Christie, Marjorie Allingham, John Dickson Carr and Leslie Charteris. There were also some Sherlock Holmes paperbacks I'd bought new and, as I moved on from murder mysteries, books by Orwell, Dickens, Trollope, Arnold Bennett, O. Henry and Somerset Maugham, plus some more recent hardbacks Judy had bought me as presents. Even the most battered specimens were precious to me and I would never have contemplated throwing them away, but neither had I thought about putting them on display. Until now.

Before embarking on my week of decorating I asked one of my neighbours, Mick at number 228, if he'd put up some bookshelves for me. Like all our neighbours, he was ingrained with a genuine sense of community. What was more, he possessed an electric drill and was pleased to have the opportunity to use it. Mick produced a simple construction: four or five metal rods attached to the wall, upon which were affixed supports for the white, laminated shelves to be laid across. He refused to accept any remuneration, so I bought him my favourite Simon and Garfunkel LP, *Bookends*, which seemed appropriate.

I can't say that my painting was as proficient as Mick's carpentry, but it was adequate. Our main living area consisted of a single room that ran from the front window to the back and served as a lounge at one end and a dining room at the other. The orange paper covered the whole lot. It took four coats of white emulsion to eradicate it completely. I also used emulsion on the ceiling and architrave and applied white gloss to all the woodwork.

For entertainment during this lonely week of hard labour I listened to music in the morning, either on Radio 1 or on Judy's English Electric record-player. In the afternoons I'd treat myself to a play on Radio 4. I'd loved radio plays since I was a child.

Our limited collection of LPs had a couple of recent additions. Judy had given me an album by the Incredible String Band for Christmas. I tried so hard to like *The 5000 Spirits or the Layers of the Onion*. I'd always been a bit of a folkie and wanted to understand why this band received such glowing reviews in the music press. On the principle that familiarity would breed content, I must have played that LP more times that week than I ever have in the ensuing forty-nine years.

While I could appreciate tracks such as 'Paint Box' and 'The Hedgehog Song', there was a pervasive tweeness that grated on me. I eventually concluded that any album that has to be forced on to the turntable is better left in its sleeve.

I was much happier with our other new acquisition, *Abbey Road*, the final album recorded by the Beatles, although not the last to be released. By the dawn of the 1970s, the end was in sight for them. Their very last album, the substandard *Let It Be*, would be launched in April, but as I listened to *Abbey Road* during my week as a painter and decorator, I knew, as everybody did, that the internal divisions within the group, and between John and Paul in particular, were leading inexorably to the break-up of the band that had changed the world.

I loved *Abbey Road*, especially the sixteen-minute medley on what I still think of as Side 2. I wasn't pleased that they too had caught the 'silly lyrics' virus. I didn't really believe that, in the end, the love you take is equal to the love you make, but hey, the overall effect of the farrago preceding the articulation of that sentiment was sublime, and those three words 'in the end' still bring tears to my eyes when I listen to the album, because it was indeed the end.

The parting of the ways was probably for the best, sad though it was. They went out in style after seven incredible years. If they'd carried on it would have been impossible to maintain the same high standards and their music would no longer have been exclusively framed by the iconoclastic sixties.

The first year of the new decade saw the release of solo albums by Paul, John and George. So, in a way, the Beatles' output trebled, although they could never be as good apart as they had been together. To a great extent due to their influence, the music scene in general had risen to new heights and there were many brilliant musicians seeking to fill the void they had left. I was largely unmoved by Hendrix and Led Zeppelin, preferring the more experimental music coming from across the Atlantic from the likes of the Mothers of Invention, the Doors, Richie Havens and the Velvet Underground, which I'd first discovered on John Peel's *Perfumed Garden* show on pirate radio and continued to access on Radio 1 after he moved to the BBC.

In Britain, Badfinger seemed worthy of the patronage Paul McCartney gave them in producing their early records. And Cat Stevens had morphed into an inspired balladeer.

Later in the year, after a particularly lucrative week of overtime, I managed to set aside enough cash to buy *After the Gold Rush*, the third solo album from Neil Young that everybody in the music press was raving about. It wasn't easy to justify such luxuries when the money could have been saved for the appliances we needed, especially when Judy was still washing all our clothes by hand for want of a washing machine and, during warm weather, our milk had to stand in a bowl of cold water in the larder for want of a fridge.

But *After the Gold Rush* was a luscious treat, and its title song was one of the first to highlight the environmental damage being done to our planet. The young Canadian singing about it would become a permanent feature of my record-buying through the years to come.

～

When Judy and the girls returned from their week away at my sister's the living–dining room had been transformed from orange to white and accessorised by my little library of books, which filled the four long shelves Mick had drilled into place.

I'd pondered various ways of breaking up the long stretch of white wall beyond the bookshelves. We had no paintings to hang from the picture rails. In one final burst of creativity, I decided to display my Spanish guitar instead.

Two electric guitars had come and gone, along with the bands I'd played in, but the battered old acoustic my mother had bought me, on which I'd practised day after day, bent over my copy of Bert Weedon's *Play in a Day*, had survived the calamities that had befallen all the rest of my instruments and equipment.

Now it had pride of place on the wall, hanging by its mock leather strap from a silver metal picture hook, where it was easily accessible whenever I wanted to play. And when I wasn't playing, there it was on full view, a constant reminder of the past and what might have been the future.

1971

A Case of You

On 10 January 1971, Judy gave birth to a plump baby boy. We'd been hoping for a son but decided we didn't want to know the sex of the baby in advance. The information was available to parents-to-be by then, though there were as yet no ultrasound photographs of the foetus to drool over.

So we had no idea whether we were to be blessed with a son or a daughter until Jamie emerged in our upstairs bedroom at Long Furlong Drive at 2.30 on a slate-grey winter morning. Both Natalie and Emma had been born in hospital, but by the early 1970s home births were being encouraged by the National Health Service and Judy was a willing volunteer, despite the potential risks of giving birth some distance away from hospital facilities. Fortunately, she had a very experienced midwife as one of the two in attendance that night.

The senior midwife was not a convert to the rapidly growing conviction that a father had every right, some would say a duty, to be present at the birth of his child. Unmoved by my attempts to charm her with tea and sycophancy, she opined in a soft

Irish accent: 'We'll all be better off, for sure, if you managed to keep a grip on your curiosity until after Baby has been born, washed and placed in its mother's arms. You wouldn't want to be getting in the way, now, would you?'

And so I was downstairs, sitting on our little two-seater sofa, as my wife and son struggled through a life-and-death drama in the room above my head. The senior midwife had, I learned later, saved the life our son had only just embarked upon when he was born with the umbilical cord wrapped tightly round his neck. It seemed he was following in my footsteps right from the start, as exactly the same thing had happened during my own birth twenty years earlier.

We'd had the name Jamie ready when Emma was born, in case she had been a boy. It was now given flesh by the crying bundle of snot presented to me by the midwives when I was finally allowed to enter the room.

Jamie was to become a terrific musician, playing guitar better than I ever could, writing songs of genuine quality and recording albums with the likes of Paul Weller, Robert Wyatt, David Gilmour and Razorlight. I feel that in some weird, primitive way I might have encouraged him down this path by writing a song for him in the hour or so after he was born.

During the period when I probably should have been doing more to help upstairs, I took down my Spanish guitar from the snow-white wall of our living room and wrote a little three-verse song entitled 'Your First Day'.

I was playing quietly, to ensure I didn't wake Natalie and Emma, who were sleeping above me – though given that they managed to sleep through the event taking place in the next room, I probably needn't have worried – but still I wonder whether perhaps this musical tribute may have been one of Jamie's first impressions of the world he'd entered. The Irish midwife who'd saved his life certainly heard me in the process of composition. When I next went upstairs with a cup of tea for Judy I was taken to one side. 'Now, haven't you got more useful things to be doing rather than plonking on that guitar, Mr Johnson?' she asked.

Some people have no sense of priorities.

∽

Although paternity leave was unheard of in 1971, I was to find myself being granted seven weeks of it, thanks to an all-out strike in the Post Office. Unfortunately it was unpaid, which made this a very difficult period in most respects, but on the plus side, as well as placing me at the disposal of my wife and baby, it allowed me to spend time with Natalie and Emma, aged four and two, when I would normally have been at work.

I'd already learned a whole repertoire of children's songs from Judy who, as a nursery nurse, had an entire back catalogue of them committed to memory. I had two favourites that the girls were obliged to sing whether they wanted to or not.

The first was 'In a Cottage in a Wood', complete with dramatic gestures and theatrical effects. ('"Help me! Help me! Help me!" he said, "Before the hunter shoots me dead. Come little rabbit, come inside, happy we shall be."') The other was 'The Wheels on the Bus Go Round and Round' which, again, was more of a performance than a song.

It was these ditties that were most important to me now, not the hit records I used to try to recreate with the Area and the In-Betweens. Sometimes I'd take down the guitar from the wall for a rendition of 'Papa's Taking Us to the Zoo Tomorrow' or 'Puff the Magic Dragon', to which the girls would sing along. My next-door neighbour, Martin, had a sweet voice and a passion for Simon and Garfunkel, and occasionally we'd sing one of their songs from *Bridge Over Troubled Water* as a duet, with me on guitar, as a party piece for the entertainment of our neighbours. It was as close as I got to a return to public performance.

We had entered the era of the singer-songwriter: a simpler, post-Beatles period in which I felt my own songs could flourish – when I had time to focus on them. Meanwhile, throughout 1971 a warm musical breeze flowed into our Slough council house from the west coast of America, on whose currents you could almost smell the marijuana. I loved the album *Déjà Vu* by Crosby, Stills, Nash and Young, released the previous year, and followed all four artists individually as well as collectively. Already a fan of Neil Young's *After the Gold Rush*, I discovered Stephen Stills's 'Love the One You're With' and a solo album by Graham Nash, a British transplant to the west coast, packed with gorgeous tunes. I also liked James Taylor, Jackson Browne and Sly and the Family Stone. But if there was one artist who made an indelible impression on me as the Post Office strike dragged on, Britain converted to decimal currency and protests against the Vietnam War intensified, and whose songs still remind me most of that time, it was Joni Mitchell.

After hearing bits of her album *Ladies of the Canyon* and seeing a TV clip of her playing 'Clouds', I was hooked. Here was somebody capable of painting vivid pictures with her lyrics and a songwriter who never lapsed into lazy self-indulgence. She was as much poet as performer and that amazing voice soared above everything, pure and crystalline.

Fortunately, the Incredible String Band experience hadn't discouraged Judy from buying albums for me and that Christmas, with the postal dispute, thankfully, long settled and Jamie approaching his first birthday, she presented me with *Blue*, Joni Mitchell's latest LP, and an album I regard as one of the finest ever made. Listening to 'A Case of You', my favourite track on this superlative record, as the year faded into memory, I felt more uxorious, more optimistic for my family's future and more convinced than ever that music was as critical to my life as the air in my lungs and the blood in my veins.

1972

Our House

ALTHOUGH WE LIVED only thirty miles outside London, the move to Slough might just as well have been to the Lake District for all the contact we had with the city of our birth. We never went back to North Kensington, venturing only as far as the outskirts of west London to visit Nan in her flat at Hanwell.

I didn't even stay in touch with the Coxes, who had so generously taken me in and shown me such kindness, let alone Sham or any of my other former bandmates in the In-Betweens. It was as if we were living a completely new life. As for relatives, Linda maintained the lines of communication with Liverpool, where we had many aunts, uncles and cousins on my mother's side, and I was happy to leave all that to her.

The only person from my past to whom I stayed close was my best friend Andrew Wiltshire. He and Ann had also left London behind and, by complete coincidence, had ended up living in the same town as Linda and Mike: Tring in rural Hertfordshire.

To be fair, it was harder then to keep in contact with distant friends and family. For those, like us, who were not 'on the phone', the only means of doing so was by letter. All my telephonic contact had to be conducted through the Inquiry Office at Slough sorting office. I used their phone so often that I still remember the number.

Andrew went through a whole series of jobs, having left the Post Office shortly after I transferred to Slough. At one point he was one of the early computer programmers, working nights, and would call the Inquiry Office at around 6am as I was preparing my early-morning delivery. The routine never varied. He would ring and simply ask whoever answered if he could speak to Alan Johnson. The Inquiry Office was on the opposite side of the vast open-plan sorting office from my delivery frame, and I would be summoned by a loud shout to come and take the call.

I'd ring Linda from there every five or six weeks before venturing forth on my second delivery. I wasn't alone in committing what I suppose was a breach of the rules. Nobody seemed to view it as any kind of offence and none of the many supervisors watching over us ever intervened. This was in the days before British Telecom was created when the telephone network was still run by the Post Office, so it seemed to me entirely reasonable that those working for the organisation should have access to free telephone calls in the same way as railway staff enjoyed free travel.

Not having a car added to my happy state of isolation, although I had begun to take advantage of another perk of being a postman (an official one): free driving lessons. As the Post Office was always short of drivers, it employed its own instructors and examiners in an effort to recruit from within.

I'd begun learning with them in London, but it would take some time (and many failed tests) before I was fully licensed.

I'd always wanted to learn to play the piano more than I wanted to learn to drive, and in 1972 I decided to do something about it. I signed up for evening classes at Slough College. I hadn't had a piano at home since Linda and I abandoned our father's old joanna to its fate at Walmer Road, so before the classes began at the start of the academic year in September, I would have to acquire one. From the classified ads in the local paper I found an old upright piano for sale at a house in Colnbrook, about eight miles away. It cost £10, plus a further £5 to have a removals firm transport it to the Britwell. And I would need to oversee the operation at both ends.

The instrument had belonged to an elderly gentleman who'd recently died, and his former home had been emptied of everything save for this piano. The estate agent who let us in pointed out that the removal men were facing a challenge: it was on the fourth floor at the top of a narrow, winding staircase.

This was a scene that could have come straight out of the 'Mr Shifter' TV ad popular at the time for PG Tips tea, in which a couple of chimpanzees, dressed up as cheery Cockney removal men, attempt to manoeuvre a piano down a flight of stairs. Inevitably, the piano comes crashing to the bottom. 'Dad, do you know the piano's on my foot?' says the younger chimp, setting up the old music-hall punchline: 'You 'um it, son, I'll play it.'

Those chimp ads apparently dated back to 1956, and they continued on and off for forty years, until changing attitudes prompted advertisers to take a fresh approach to appeal to a new generation of tea-drinkers who were less amused by the idea of live chimps dressed up as humans.

I remember once reading a report concerning a question in Parliament on the issue of the welfare of the TV chimps. The MP who raised it asked the minister how he'd like to be a monkey in a PG Tips commercial. To which another honourable member shouted: 'He is!'

As my two intrepid removal men in Colnbrook scratched their chins and considered the logistics of their task, I couldn't help thinking about those chimps and fervently hoping my piano wasn't going to meet the same fate as theirs. The chin-rubbing only lasted a minute or two before a plan was made and the men began the delicate operation of getting the piano down four flights of stairs, through a narrow passage and out to the van.

Their *modus operandi* was to turn the piano and place it gently on one end, so that it became a tall load rather than a wide one. One of the removal men then positioned himself on a lower step while his colleague held the top. The piano was rested on the first man's back and he set off backwards down the stairs like a crab carrying a tree stump. It was a remarkable display of skill and dexterity executed without fuss or drama.

At the other end there were no stairs involved and it was comparatively easy to get the piano through the front door and lug it into our living room, where it was positioned against the white wall, in the spot where the sofa had been, beneath my picture-hooked guitar. In a burst of innovation, I painted it white.

We managed to get the man who tuned the piano at St George's Church over the road to come round and tune ours, and that was me ready. My mission to be in possession of a fully functioning piano before starting my lessons had been accomplished.

What I really wanted was to learn how to play rock 'n' roll piano; to vamp, to boogie-woogie; to be as conversant with chords on the keyboard as I was on the guitar. Alas, such a course wasn't available. All that was on offer at Slough College was the traditional Royal College of Music piano grades. We were to be taught classical piano with the aim of securing Grades 1 and 2 (which, confusingly, are the lowest levels of competence, Grade 8 being the highest).

On the first Tuesday evening twenty of us gathered for our opening two-hour lesson but by the third week that number had halved to the ten dauntless souls who intended to see the course through to its conclusion the following spring.

Of the Tenacious Ten I was one of only two men and, if the class were to be analysed by 'class', the only participant from the proletariat. As if to prove the point, I turned up most weeks in my Post Office uniform, though there was no ulterior motive involved – I just didn't have time to change after work. The college was only a five-minute walk from the sorting office on Wellington Street, but it was still a rush to get there on time.

None of my classmates were from the Britwell or the other huge council estate on the other side of Slough, the Trelawney. I record this merely as an observation. No snobbery was directed towards me, nor was I made to feel uncomfortable in any way. After all, the whole purpose of adult education was to give those who'd left school without achieving much a second chance. In general, though, it seemed to me that the courses were populated largely by those who had plenty of qualifications already and were simply seeking recreation. On this course the distinction was irrelevant. If you hadn't learned to play the piano in childhood, whatever your upbringing, it was a marvellous opportunity to rectify the omission. The lessons weren't free, but neither were they expensive.

The term 'beginners' covered a broad range of experience. Some of the women had learned to play the piano as children but had allowed their skills to lapse in adulthood. They were all in their forties or fifties. The only other male student, Roger, could already read music very well. He played clarinet to a decent standard but had never mastered the piano and, like the rest of us, badly wanted to do so.

We all noticed very early on that Roger had become particularly friendly with Jan, an attractive blonde from Farnham Common. Indeed, by Christmas we suspected that Jan and Roger were enjoying more than music together. They always sat close to one another and Jan was becoming increasingly distant from Rita, the friend with whom she'd begun coming to the classes.

I couldn't testify to the marital status of either Roger or Jan, but they both wore wedding rings and they certainly weren't married to each other. It would be unfair to accuse me or the rest of the class of prurience. Within a small group, thrown together for a couple of hours every week, in which people are forced to demonstrate their proficiency (or lack of it) in front of one another on a regular basis, a certain camaraderie is forged and a change in the intensity of relationships is invariably noticeable. We weren't passing judgement, just registering the demonstrable gestures of affection: the stroking of an arm, shared conspiratorial laughter, congratulatory hugs that went on for just that little bit too long after a piece had been played particularly well.

As is so often the case with office romances, the surprising thing is not that such dalliances are quickly rumbled but how secret lovers manage to persuade themselves that they are being discreet when their behaviour constantly gives the game away. They giggle and gush to such an extent that they might just as well have labels on their foreheads saying, 'We're having it off.'

At our last lesson before Christmas there was German wine and mince pies and we all took turns at playing 'When the Saints Go Marching In'. Rita seemed more estranged from Jan than ever and, when we all trooped over to the pub for a Christmas drink afterwards, she declined to join us. Roger sat with his arm round Jan as we exchanged the compliments of the season and anticipated the new term that would begin in January.

We never saw Roger or Jan again. When lessons resumed I heard Rita whispering to some of the other women in the class and picked up enough to deduce that the affair had been either discovered or admitted over the Christmas break. I have no idea what the ramifications were for their relationship or whatever marriages were caught up in it, but through Rita's pursed lips came the implication that the little drama played out in our piano lessons had ended badly. Whatever the case, the upshot for me was that I saw out the year as the lone male among the eight survivors.

I think I passed Grades 1 and 2 that year, but whatever certificates I may have had I don't have now, so I can't be sure. The tutor encouraged me to progress through the grades but told me I must focus on reading the music rather than playing from memory. I knew this was my greatest weakness. I had no wish to read music, just to play the piano. I reasoned that if I could transfer the chords I played on the guitar to the right-hand keyboard part, and muck about on the bass notes with my left, I could be as good a pianist as I wanted to be without slogging over the classical pieces at evening class.

At home, the Crosby, Stills, Nash and Young album *Déjà Vu*, the first to feature all four of them, was still regularly placed on our turntable. We were not alone in loving that record. It was a huge commercial success that has stood the test of time – today its cumulative sales have topped eight million. Judy and I were especially fond of 'Our House', one of the two Graham Nash songs on the album (the other is 'Teach Your Children', originally written when he was with the Hollies, though they never made a studio recording of it).

I had the sheet music for 'Our House' and decided to try to read the piano lines on the basis of what I'd been taught at evening class. On guitar it was basically the A and D chords with variations and I found the translation to piano worked well. This moderate success wrongly convinced me that I'd learned as much as I needed to learn at my piano lessons.

On this basis I decided not to continue with evening classes. I took them up again twenty years later at another college in Croydon, and since then I've even had some one-to-one tuition, but I still haven't learned to play the piano. At least, not yet.

1973

Starman

I N MY TEENS I believed that a person passed irretrievably into old age when they could no longer name the record at the top of the hit parade. Those lost souls who were never able to name a Number 1 even in their youth were irrelevant to my theory. They represented a sad minority to be pitied rather than pilloried. Having never experienced the joy of pop music they were, in effect, born middle-aged.

As for the rest of us, those with a normal healthy interest in what was going up or coming down the charts, who turned on *Top of the Pops* religiously every Thursday evening and tuned into Radio 1 on Sunday afternoons to hear the week's newly minted chart, it was inconceivable that any of us would ever not possess, or not want to possess, such crucial knowledge.

I now accept that this is a state of being that comes to us all eventually, like listening to *Gardeners' Question Time* and wearing a cardigan. But I didn't expect it to hit me as soon as it did. I would date the start of that loss of interest to 1973, though it wasn't immediate. It came upon me gradually, insidiously, until, when somebody asked me one day if I liked the artist who had just reached Number 1, I looked blank, and even blanker when I was told who it was.

Of course, losing interest in the charts is not the same as losing interest in music. Now the charts are a diminished force it is is hard to convey a sense of the importance they once had. However, they were never an exact science. In the early 1960s individual music papers compiled their own, and the BBC would use an amalgamation of them all to produce their chart. This threw up the odd celebrated anomaly, such as Frank Ifield's 'Wayward Wind' unaccountably keeping 'Please Please Me' by the Beatles from the top spot in 1963.

And as the decade wore on, and the record companies worked out which shops were being used to submit their sales figures, they employed all sorts of tricks to promote their own records, from doorstepping DJs to try to persuade them to add a single to their playlists, or sending junior staff round London with a fistful of fivers to buy up stock in the key shops, to outright bribery, tempting shop workers with T-shirts or badges, sometimes even a bottle of whisky, to add more copies to their sales figures.

By the beginning of the 1970s, albums were more popular, outselling singles by almost two to one. The singles charts still mattered, and young music fans still really cared about their favourite artist getting to Number 1, but a growing preference for LPs over singles was usually the reason why record-buyers who had waved goodbye to their teenage years started to drift away from a slavish devotion to the charts, as was the case with me.

The last 45rpm record I ever bought was 'Rocket Man' by Elton John in 1972, which I decided was needed to add a more contemporary feel to our record collection for a party. The young families living in our corner of Long Furlong Drive would take turns to host the others every four months or so and our turn had come round. Ten singles stacked on the record-player was still the most common way for party music to be provided. The more expensive LPs were jealously guarded and rarely allowed out of their sleeves at these gatherings. Getting a splash of Watney's Party Seven on one's copy of *Tubular Bells* could ruin the evening. Singles were more robust and less valued. Nobody worried if they were blemished by beer stains or discoloured by the odd dash of Martini.

By 1973 I knew what the Top 10 albums were but was less interested in which single was Number 1. For good or ill, I was maturing into advanced adulthood, but there was one last youthful musical crush to get out of my system before I attained it. As a small boy I'd revered Lonnie Donegan; in my teens I wanted to be Paul McCartney. Now, in my twenties, I'd become a full-blown Bowie freak.

After being attracted in 1969 to 'Space Oddity', in 1971 I'd bought the *Hunky Dory* album, growing my hair to match the way Bowie wore his on the sleeve and raving about 'Changes' and 'Life on Mars'. The following year Bowie was performing as his androgynous alter ego Ziggy Stardust and by 1973, when his sixth album was released, Ziggy had developed into Aladdin Sane. The record cover depicted Bowie sporting shorter, spikier hair and the face markings that were quickly copied by his followers.

I remember a teenage postman in Slough coming on duty with that Aladdin Sane lightning bolt painted across his face and immediately being sent home to wash it off. I wasn't yet a union rep, but if I had been I'd have made a staunch defence of a man's right to paint his face. There again, I suppose I must concede that answering the postman's knock early in the morning to find a guy with an orange and blue lightning flash zigzagging down his face asking for a signature might have been a disconcerting experience for our customers.

Every Friday lunchtime five or six of us Burnham postmen would gather at the Lynchpin pub on the edge of the Britwell estate for a pint or two. Friday was pay day, and our wages, signed for that morning, still protruded in their entirety from the small brown paper envelopes in which they had been received.

There was a jukebox in the Lynchpin which contained Bowie's 'Starman' and its 'B' side, 'Suffragette City', from his Ziggy Stardust period. I spent many a shilling piece (as we still called the new 5p coins) listening to both sides during our sojourns in the pub. I would even have my older workmates joining in the 'Wham bam, thank you ma'am' climax of 'Suffragette City' by the end of the session.

'Starman' carved a niche for itself in pop history for the way Bowie performed the song on *Top of the Pops* in 1972. In those innocent days his androgynous appearance, professed bisexuality and cavorting with Mick Ronson, the extravagantly talented lead guitarist of his band, the Spiders From Mars, were enough to create a huge scandal. Some of the guys at work swore blind they'd seen the two men kiss. With home videorecorders not generally available, let alone remotely within the means of the average consumer, until well into the 1980s, there was no such thing as a replay. If you missed a moment on television, you missed it, and even when you saw it, you had your own perception, and your own memory, of what you'd seen.

Such was the autosuggestive power of repetition that it wasn't long before I became convinced myself that the myth about the kiss was true.

Fanning the dying embers of my youthful desire to be a non-conformist, the 'Starman' controversy only increased my admiration for Bowie. I so wanted to display my allegiance by getting Judy to use her considerable artistic skills to paint me into character as Aladdin Sane. But I was married with three children. Responsibility held me down like a pin through a mounted butterfly. My face remained unpainted.

~

I made a big decision in 1973. I suppose I had come to terms with reality. I was probably never going to play in a group again, let alone worry the pop charts. It was time to concentrate on moving forward in the life I was living, not the one I might have lived; time to seek promotion. The route up through the Post Office ranks was pre-set and could not be altered or accelerated. In the entire nineteen years I spent as a postman, no manager at any level ever encouraged me to go for promotion. The process of advancement was self-regulated and governed by seniority. It was therefore length of service, not merit, that would determine whether and when I could take the first step of becoming a postman higher grade (PHG), as Sham had done in north London.

This arbitrary system was at least even-handed. Postal workers from ethnic minorities, like Sham, moved up through the ranks as quickly as everyone else once they had a few years' service under their belts. They didn't suffer the same discrimination in the Post Office, in this respect, at least, that they would have encountered in some other occupations.

Having acquired sufficient seniority, I went for my fortnight's training to be a PHG (the grade that dealt with minor clerical duties and specialised sorting) and then joined an 'acting list', which did not mean becoming a thespian, just that my name would be on the list of postmen who had completed training and were available to gain experience by covering absences while waiting for a PHG vacancy to arise. Each rung on the ladder up towards the heady ranks of the postal executives (salaried senior managers) had to be taken in this way. If I started climbing now, I could reach the highest rung in ten years' time.

It was a difficult decision for me to make because I so enjoyed the job I was doing already. As a postman, I was working outdoors, largely unsupervised; as a PHG I would be indoors. But a PHG's wages were 15 per cent higher than a postman's and I needed both to earn more money and to consider the future. I didn't want to be working seventy-hour weeks into my dotage. I didn't much fancy becoming a manager but the fact was, if I didn't first apply for a PHG position, I would never have the choice. None of the stages could be leapfrogged.

So it was that by December I was working as an 'acting PHG' on the Outward Section of Slough sorting office, which handled mail posted in Slough for delivery elsewhere. Every Christmas the Post Office changed utterly. From late November the entire operation switched to 'Christmas Pressure' mode in preparation for the enormous influx of cards and parcels that would overwhelm the system in the run-up to the festive season.

Into our ranks marched an army of Christmas casuals, most of them students looking to earn extra money in the vacation.

There was also a large contingent of wives and girlfriends of our predominantly male workforce, plus retired ex-employees tempted back by the prospect of supplementing their pensions.

Regular staff in Slough had their attendances altered to a compulsory twelve-hour daily shift, with Sunday included as a normal working day. Additional sorting frames were constructed and an extra fleet of vehicles hired. The influx of so many students brought down the average age of the workforce by at least a generation and the arrival of so many women made for a more diverse and colourful workplace.

Christmas was a jolly time to be a postman, though it must be said that the jovial atmosphere was due at least in part to the chaos that reigned during those weeks. The supervisors had no idea where the regular staff were, let alone where they were supposed to be. Space on the huge sorting-office floor was suddenly at a premium, the noise and bustle intensified and, in the most revolutionary departure from normality, radios blared out music day and night.

In 1973, down on the Outward Section, every one of the millions of letters we processed had to be sorted by hand. Alphanumeric postcodes were yet to be applied to every address in the UK so automated sorting was still a few years away.

My job that Christmas was to stack the sorting frames with letters. Despite my 'higher grade' and my pay rise I was employed basically as a manual labourer, lifting trays of 'faced' mail (letters that had been arranged the same way up, with the stamp in the top-right corner) and lugging them to the sorting frames, where I'd lay them out in front of the sorters, crammed together like battery hens waiting to be fed.

There was much banter, some interesting conversation and

even a bit of mild flirting. I remember one stunningly attractive woman who worked as what was then known as a ground hostess, taking care of passengers before they boarded their flights, at Heathrow airport, just off the next junction down the M4. Heathrow was so close that we liked to refer to it as Slough airport. Don't ask me why this woman spent a fortnight in December as a Post Office casual. It's possible the pay wasn't so good at Heathrow and she had to moonlight, but she didn't seem to be short of a bob or two.

One day I asked her about the swanky vintage car I'd seen her drive into the staff car park. She told me it was an Austin. 'Ah, that would be an Austin Tatious,' I quipped, flashing my most winning smile. 'No,' she replied impassively. 'It's an A40 Sports.' I moved on quickly.

My partner on this cushy Christmas duty was one of the most senior PHGs, 'Buck' Butler, whose nickname derived from his love of cowboy films. Nobody knew his real first name. Buck's regular job was to oversee the telegram boys, but from 6pm, when the Telegram Office closed, he joined me to lend a hand through the busiest period of the day as the evening collections came in.

After the initial surge had been dealt with, Buck saw no point in us tripping over one another and insisted I go for an extended dinner break. I think I was entitled to thirty minutes, but with Buck's active connivance this could be stretched to ninety.

Every evening I'd nip across to the Rose and Crown in Slough High Street, otherwise known as the Postman's Retreat. The little snug at the back was full of postal workers – night staff on the way in, fortifying themselves before their shifts, and day staff unwinding with a swift pint before heading home.

In normal circumstances I would have worried about the overseer, the manager in ultimate control of the whole sorting office and everybody in it. But he was in the Rose and Crown as well. In fact, I distinctly remember him offering to buy me a drink one evening. It would have been rude not to accept.

The song that dominated the whole of that Christmas Pressure period, the pubs, the sorting office, everywhere, was 'Merry Xmas Everybody' by Slade. It rang around the Outward and Inward sorting frames and had the regulars, the casuals, the students and old-timers like Buck singing along. By now many people will be heartily sick of this raucous anthem as it eats into its fifth decade of Christmas ubiquity. But back then it was fresh, full of energy and ebullience, and I was twenty-three years of age with so much to look forward to.

On Christmas Eve even more postmen than usual were packed into the Rose and Crown at lunchtime. The 'Pressure' was over and we had two days' holiday ahead of us. A constant stream of 5p pieces went into the jukebox and 'Merry Xmas Everybody' was played again and again, punctuated occasionally by Wizzard's 'I Wish It Could Be Christmas Every Day'.

There is one of those little video clips of memory from that Christmas Eve in the Rose and Crown that replays in my mind with great clarity. Along with my comrades, I am lifting my pint glass joyously towards the ceiling at Noddy Holder's exhortation to look to the future which, for me that year, really had 'only just begun'.

Everybody knew which record was Number 1 in the charts that Christmas.

1974

Band on the Run

THE 1970s ARE dubbed by some 'the decade style forgot'. Certainly 1974 was a fallow year for music. Towering platform shoes and flares were everywhere, glam rock was at its zenith and Gary Glitter, Sweet and Mud dominated the charts, along with some more eccentric acts such as Showaddywaddy and the Wombles. At our Long Furlong Drive parties it was inevitable that some couples would do that curious non-dance that involved standing rooted to the spot and swaying their shoulders down towards one another in a rhythmic manner. I can't remember what it was called, if it had a name, but it was closely associated with Gary Glitter (with whom nobody would want to be remotely associated today).

There was only one musical highlight for me but it was a significant one. I'd followed both Paul McCartney and John Lennon into their solo careers. McCartney's first eponymous album, released in 1970, was impressive but seemed improvised and under-produced. Perhaps that was the idea: to strip everything back to basics. The second, *Ram*, was better. His first two albums with Wings, however, were a disappointment.

Then came *Band on the Run*, released in December 1973. I did not buy it until February the following year, taking the whole family to Maidenhead on a dreary Saturday for that specific purpose. Steve Coogan, in the guise of Alan Partridge, joked that 'Wings were the band the Beatles could have been.' Satire aside, *Band on the Run* is an LP the Beatles could have recorded, though they would have improved on it in the process. With only ten tracks, it was a little stingy by Beatles standards, but they were good tracks, every one of them. If a great album has to grab your attention from the start, none has done it better than *Band on the Run*, with the dynamic impact of its title track sustained by the next one, 'Jet'.

Shortly after investing in McCartney's latest project, I purchased a brand-new guitar (although the two events were not connected). My brother-in-law, Mike, who had begun to sell a few musical instruments at Henry's Radios, the electrical shop he ran, told me he could arrange a 50 per cent discount on the price of my chosen model. I surprised myself by opting for an acoustic twelve-string. I blame a folk trio called the Rooftop Singers, who'd had a hit in the early sixties with 'Walk Right In'. I'd always liked the sound of the twelve-string lead on that record, and in the expectation that I'd never be playing in a band again, I went acoustic rather than electric – a kind of reverse Dylan.

It was a lovely instrument, an Eko, made of Italian rosewood, but it was unsuitable for many of the songs I played and difficult to keep in tune. Foolishly, once this new guitar was in place, I gave my old Spanish guitar to a workmate whose son was keen to learn to play. All those memories, the sentimental value of a guitar on which I'd taught myself to play, its connection to my mother – gone with one rash decision. I regretted it immediately and thereafter, irrationally, somehow held it against the twelve-string, harbouring a baseless resentment towards my new guitar for having the temerity to usurp the one I'd treasured since childhood.

~

By now I'd passed my driving test (at the fifth attempt) and was on my third car, a sky-blue Ford Escort. It was only a year old but had already clocked up 20,000 miles when I bought it.

Judy and I had been forced to break our golden rule of never going into debt, but after two old Ford Anglias (the little cars with the curious inward sloping back window, described as 'swept back'), we needed a reliable vehicle. I'd got the first Anglia for nothing, and the second only cost us £45. A decent car required a bigger investment. Our only option, we concluded, was to resort to the dreaded 'never-never'.

Having a car ended our geographic isolation. We could get to see friends and relatives more easily and it enriched our cultural lives by enabling us to make the trip to London more often to see a show.

Our circle of friends in Slough consisted of couples like us with small children, most of them neighbours in Long Furlong Drive. The most socially adventurous were Dave and Pauline Henshaw, who lived on the other side of Slough. Dave was a postman at the tiny sorting office in Iver and played with me for the Post Office football team. Pauline had football connections as well: her cousin Joe Laidlaw played professionally for Middlesbrough. So whenever QPR were at home to Boro, I was able to get good tickets in the stands from Dave.

With Dave and Pauline we widened our horizons. There were outings to Windsor theatre, to Caesar's Palace in Luton and the Shaftesbury theatre in the West End where, in the early 1970s, we'd seen the rock musical *Hair*. The famous nude scene at the end of Act 1 was so fleeting, and the stage so dark, that the age of Aquarius failed to dawn for us that evening. However, I just loved the soundtrack, particularly 'Frank Mills' (performed years later as a great rock song by the Lemonheads), 'Let the Sunshine In' and 'Good Morning Starshine'.

In 1974 somebody (it might have been me) suggested a trip to the Duchess theatre in London to see *Oh! Calcutta!* While we liked to think of ourselves as broadminded representatives of our generation, none of us had ever seen a show that could boast two exclamation marks in its title.

Judy and I, Dave and Pauline, and Mick and Sandra from three doors down decided, with no cultural pretensions whatsoever, that we would go. We were just keen to be shocked. From the vantage point of today's world, our prurience must seem almost quaint. But this was 1974 and Kenneth Tynan's avant-garde revue offered not only nudity but profanity as well.

Dave hired a minibus for the night, and in the end there were eight of us on board after Pauline invited her elderly parents (well, we considered them elderly – they were probably only in their late fifties). Her mother even came equipped with opera glasses to get a better view. Strangely, I can remember nothing about the performance. Devoid of the great tunes that made *Hair* memorable, this show did shock, but that was all it did. It lacked even a trace of wit. We were almost unanimous in pronouncing it tedious and eminently forgettable, except for Pauline's mum, who thought it was 'interesting'.

After the show we went to a restaurant called Flanagan's, one of a chain with an Edwardian music-hall theme. There was sawdust on the floor and a honky-tonk pianist playing in one corner. He was a big man in a canary yellow jacket whose wide, fat face was sweating profusely.

We were only too conscious of this because our table was right next to him in the packed restaurant. Every so often he'd take out the handkerchief hanging from the breast pocket of his garish jacket and use it to mop the sweat from his brow with one hand while continuing to play with the other. After a tune or two he'd burst into the restaurant's signature song and his audience would dutifully sing along: 'Flanagan, Flanagan, take me to the Isle of Man again . . .' The words of this and other ditties were printed on the paper napkins.

Carried away by the atmosphere, the wine and my natural propensity to show off, in the middle of the chorus I lifted the pianist's boater, which was lying open side up next to him on the long piano stool, and placed it on my head. Unbeknown to me, it was full of the coins he had collected as tips throughout a busy evening. As this small fortune scattered into the sawdust the pianist, still playing and smiling, leaned towards me and said softly: 'If you don't get down on all fours and retrieve every fucking penny, I'll wring your fucking neck, you stupid little bastard.'

Profanity on the stage was one thing, but I felt this had a rather unnecessary personal edge to it.

1975

Born to Run

IT COULD BE said that I was involved in the negotiations which took Britain into what was then the European Community (and what would become the European Union). This may be a slight exaggeration, but it happened like this.

I had been elected to the Postmen's Committee of the Slough Amalgamated Branch of the Union of Post Office Workers (UPW) in 1974, only to find that I was a member of a committee that never met. The names of the ten members, including mine, were displayed on the UPW noticeboard in the sorting office so that the members who'd ostensibly elected us could seek our assistance in resolving whatever workplace problem they wanted a union representative to assist them with. In reality it was a rarity for any election to take place, the committee usually consisting of the last men to back away when volunteers were called for.

In the run-up to the great referendum that would decide whether Britain would remain in the European Community it had only recently joined, to be held on 5 June 1975, I was working on 'the rurals'. This was a corner of the vast sorting office from which the deliveries for Slough's surrounding villages were prepared and dispatched. Pottering around the Bucks and Berks countryside in a Royal Mail van conferred a status and a job satisfaction that couldn't be achieved by pedalling a bike on the town deliveries, and the men on these 'walks' formed a senior elite who'd spurned promotion in favour of using their seniority to secure the most desirable routes in the more attractive locations.

As yet no PHG vacancies had come up for me, and with seven years' service I had enough seniority to get on to a Farnham Common rural delivery temporarily while I was waiting.

One morning in May we arrived at work to find stacks of unaddressed leaflets piled high on the racks above our delivery frames. The supervisors told us that these were circulars setting out the case for and against remaining in the European Community. Others would follow, including one from Her Majesty's government. We were to integrate these handouts with our normal stamped mail over the next couple of weeks. So as not to incur any overtime, the supervisors exhorted us to 'take them where you're going', in other words, to those addresses for which there was already a stamped letter to deliver. They were making the reasonable assumption that every address would meet this criterion at least once over the next fortnight.

The reaction among the rural men was mutinous. This was akin to ordering an elite company of Roman legionnaires to do a spot of knitting.

We were postmen paid to deliver the Queen's mail, not distributors of leaflets. That was women's work. It would be fair to say that by the time I arrived at the office, half an hour late, as usual, the dudgeon in which I found the men was extremely high.

I had received no training in any aspect of being a union rep, let alone in what to do in a situation such as this, where the supervisors were insisting that the leaflets must be delivered and the men were adamantly refusing. The branch secretary, who was the chief local negotiator, was on office hours. By the time he arrived at work, the men might have walked out or been suspended from duty, such was the strength of feeling.

I swallowed hard, demanded to see the senior office manager on duty and was ushered into the presence of a meticulously groomed former sergeant-major by the name of Frank Taylor. Frank, like everyone in management, had once been a postman himself. He asked me what credentials I had to represent the rural postmen. I referred him to the list of committee members on the UPW noticeboard, which seemed to satisfy him. He sat me down in his office and closed the door. Frank was twice my age and had the thinnest of moustaches to match his military bearing. There was a twinkle in his eye as he gazed upon the innocent novice who'd entered his lair.

'Now, Alan, perhaps you'd explain why the rurals, who all have the luxury of a van to carry the mail, are so outraged when the town men, who have to carry theirs on a bike, seem perfectly content to take these leaflets where they are going,' he said.

I'd anticipated this distinction being commented on, and by the time Mr Taylor and I met at 6am, the two hundred or so town postmen had been stirred into a similar state of outrage.

'I am here on behalf of all the delivery staff, Mr Taylor,' I replied nervously, 'and none of them, town or rural, is satisfied with this "take them where you're going" instruction.'

As it was essential that these things were delivered well before the 5 June referendum, I knew I had a strong hand to play. Furthermore, since Post Office wages in the booming Thames Valley were uncompetitive and Slough was always short of staff, the goodwill of the men was a crucial component of getting through each working day.

I had a proposition ready to resolve the situation and Frank and I did a deal of which I like to think the prime minister, Harold Wilson, who had been engaged in negotiations in Brussels to improve the terms of British membership prior to the referendum, would have approved. Each complete leaflet delivery would attract an overtime payment of three hours, irrespective of whether or not the hours were worked.

I think there were four of these handouts in total: a 'yes' leaflet, a 'no' leaflet, the government's recommendation and one from the opposition Conservative party, whose new leader, Margaret Thatcher, was fiercely in favour of Britain's membership. (The governing Labour party was split on the issue and had decided not to campaign.)

This meant that twelve hours' overtime were available to every postman as a boost to his weekly wages in exchange for delivering the extra items within normal duty hours. In putting forward this offer, I described it as a 'productivity bonus'. I'd asked for four hours and allowed Frank to bargain me down to the three I wanted.

Thirty minutes later, the matter was settled. I returned to the 'rurals' like Lech Walesa returning to the shipyards of Gdansk having secured victory over a totalitarian regime.

~

One of my colleagues as a rural postman was Brian Tidman, a wryly humorous man about a decade older than me. Brian was a fellow music enthusiast and always seemed to be one step ahead of me in his familiarity with the latest rock sensation from America. He it was who introduced me to the Eagles (I had a lot of time for the Eagles, but I could never match his devotion to the band because their albums featured so many make-weight tracks that were utter dross).

In 1975 he lent me a record by a US artist who almost justified the incredible hype that surrounded him. Apparently, Columbia Records spent a quarter of a million dollars promoting *Born to Run* by Bruce Springsteen. This seemed plausible: long before I'd heard any of Springsteen's music, I'd read articles in the music press, and even in Sunday newspaper supplements, hailing him as the 'new Bob Dylan' and, somewhat bizarrely, 'the future of rock'.

Brian wanted us to go with our wives when Bruce and the E Street Band played the Hammersmith Odeon, but for some reason I declined. It was a decision I came to regret because when I saw footage of Springsteen's concerts later, it became clear that I'd missed an opportunity to experience a show by one of the greatest live performers in rock history. Bruce Springsteen wasn't the future of rock but, in my view, he was and remains one of its greatest practitioners. And at a time when music was drifting towards elaborate over-production, he represented a return to its raw and exciting past.

Unfortunately Springsteen didn't make it to Slough, but the biggest British pop group of the era did – to the Holiday Inn on the London Road, Langley. I'm not sure why the Bay City Rollers came to my town. They certainly weren't performing there.

Slough didn't have a venue big enough to accommodate the Rollers. Most likely they were staying there overnight before an early-morning flight from Heathrow.

Pundits claimed that the Bay City Rollers were responsible for a 1970s version of Beatlemania but this was a specious comparison. A more accurate one would have been with the Monkees, the manufactured sixties band who had their hits written for them and appealed almost exclusively to a very young female audience.

That's not to decry either the Rollers or the Monkees. They were both authentic pop phenomena who sold an extraordinary number of records (120 million in the case of the Bay City Rollers). But pop music aficionados grew weary of the constant predictions that every successful band that came along was going to be bigger than the Beatles. Such a band never materialised.

In the spring of 1975 the boys with the calf-length tartan-edged trousers and tartan scarves were carrying all before them. They were Number 1 in the charts with the old Four Seasons hit 'Bye Bye Baby', they had their own television programme (called *Shang-a-Lang*) and were conquering countries all around the globe.

I seem to remember that their stay at the Holiday Inn was meant to be a secret but it seemed a chambermaid couldn't resist telling her friends. Despite the absence of social media in those far-off days, this kind of news always spread faster than a virulent epidemic.

My colleagues in the sorting office reported seeing legions of young girls gravitating towards and congregating outside the newly built hotel. I had a direct interest in this intelligence as I was scheduled to do the Langley collection that evening, and one of the pillarboxes I had to clear was only a few metres from the hotel.

By the time I reached the London Road at about 6.15pm there was a police cordon outside the hotel and the multitude of girls being penned back into the area around my pillarbox must have numbered a couple of thousand. The crowd was dense and boisterous. There was even a girl sitting on top of the pillarbox. The main road had been reduced to a single lane and I couldn't get my van anywhere near the box. Pushing through this throng with my sack and big bunch of keys would have been hard enough; the chances of opening the box, clearing the mail and getting back to the van were more or less zero. I calculated that to attempt it would have constituted a risk to life and limb.

As this was the final port of call on my collection, I turned the van round and headed straight back to the sorting office, leaving the pillarbox unopened. The supervisor in charge that evening was Lenny Hayes, a big, rollicking Cockney who fully justified the over-used accolade 'larger than life'. Len was an avid Arsenal supporter who had a unique matchday quirk which I discovered when he came to QPR with me for (I think) an FA Cup replay. Len would light a cigarette immediately the game kicked off and smoke continuously throughout the match. As the final whistle blew, he would stub out his latest fag, irrespective of how far through smoking it he was, and not touch another one until the start of the next game, when the whole business would be repeated.

As he was an Arsenal season-ticket-holder and attended many away matches as well, this was not an inexpensive habit.

I calculated that even if each cigarette took as long as five minutes to smoke, he'd be getting through a packet of twenty at every game. I thought that perhaps he was a former smoker who'd given up but couldn't help backsliding during an absorbing match, but Len told me he had never smoked in his life, except at the football. He claimed it helped him cope with the stress.

When I reported my inability to get to the London Road pillarbox, Len's response was theatrical. Sounding like Sir Laurence Olivier in *Henry V*, he held court loudly in the middle of the sorting-office floor, railing against the army of girls who were preventing the Queen's mail from getting through (which was inaccurate in any case, since the mail was being prevented from coming out, not getting through) and pledging to rectify the situation personally. If there had been a horse nearby, I'm sure Len would have leaped upon it. As it was, he collared me to drive back out to the Holiday Inn with him on board, loins girded for the struggle ahead.

When he saw the crowd, which had swelled even further since my last visit, Len sat back in the passenger seat, swearing softly to himself. It looked as if every girl under sixteen from Berkshire, Buckinghamshire and Middlesex was outside that hotel. Len didn't lack courage. Taking a deep breath, he jumped out of the van, in his shirtsleeves and tie, and plunged into the throng, singling out the big metal key from the bunch he held in one giant paw and clutching a dusty grey post sack in the other.

I waited in the van with the engine running, watching Big Lenny's head bobbing around. Then it disappeared from view. Ten minutes later he returned, shirt rumpled, tie askew and mail sack still empty. As I turned the van round and headed back to the sorting office, he recounted dejectedly how, as he'd inched his way towards the pillarbox through a mass of humanity denser than any he'd ever experienced at a football match, a girl shouted that she thought she'd caught sight of Woody, the Rollers' guitarist, on the balcony of one of the rooms. The crowd surged, the screaming rose in pitch and volume and Lenny, carried away from the pillarbox on the tide, made the sensible decision that he'd like to see his wife and kids again. He deserted the battlefield, mission aborted.

Len was unusually quiet during the drive. I lit a cigarette and asked him if he wanted one. To my amazement, he accepted. Rollermania must have been the only thing Len Hayes ever experienced that was more stressful than watching Arsenal.

~

Later in the year, in the inauspicious surroundings of the Scout hut on Long Furlong Drive, where Judy had organised a fund-raising disco for her playgroup, I first heard one of the most remarkable singles in pop history.

'Bohemian Rhapsody' sounded like three or four different songs thrown together by someone who'd forgotten to add a chorus. I was never that bothered whether Scaramouche did the fandango or not, and found Queen's greatest hit easy to admire but difficult to love. However, there was no denying the record's profound impact, or its innovativeness; like 'Good Vibrations', 'Strawberry Fields' and 'River Deep, Mountain High', it was destined from the start to be played for as long as records are listened to.

It was, though, prog rock's last stand, the epitome of the grandeur and pretentiousness of a genre that led almost directly to the rise of its antithesis – punk rock, and its new model army of followers.

1976

The Boys Are Back in Town

WE CAN ALL divide our lives into various phases. I have a pre-diary phase and a post-diary phase. For Christmas 1975 Judy bought me three presents: a watch, *The Oxford Book of English Verse* and a Boots page-a-day diary for 1976.

I'd been banging on for ages about the Victorians' fascination with keeping journals and how intrigued I was by their dictum that a day unrecorded was a day not lived. These not-so-subtle hints had the desired effect and I got the Christmas present I wanted.

Judy also bought a diary for herself, but the historical novels she read at bedtime soon regained ascendancy over the chore of writing up the events of the last twenty-four hours. I don't think hers made it to the end of that year. By contrast, her gift to me was the start of a pursuit that has lasted to this day, although the gaps between entries have become progressively longer. The habit is now so entrenched that I doubt if I could stop even if I wanted to.

In 1976, every day is recorded meticulously, together with

contemporary jokes that took my fancy (Question: Who was born in a barn and had millions of followers? Answer: Red Rum) and snatches of original doggerel:

> There was a young chap named Perce,
> Who just couldn't finish a verse,
> He'd start many times,
> Complete four lines,
> And end with . . .

Coincidentally, another new chapter of my life began at around the same time. As a result my transition to union official is fully recorded at the start of my 1976 diary. I was already on the Postmen's Committee, and had been for two years, but as no meetings were held, apart from my intervention on behalf of the 'rurals' the previous year, there had been no representative functions to perform.

My diary entry for Friday, 2 January reports one of my Asian colleagues, K. K. Sharma, imploring me to put my name forward for the post of branch chairman at the AGM to be held in a few weeks' time. Evidently I followed his advice, because on Sunday, 8 February I record: 'Victory in the union elections.'

I was now responsible for protecting the union rights and privileges of the 700 postmen, clerical staff, telephonists, cleaners and catering workers in Slough, Gerrard's Cross and Iver, as well as being (with the branch secretary) one of the two principal negotiating officers of the Slough Amalgamated Branch of the Union of Post Office Workers. I was twenty-five years of age and from that moment on would be subject to election and re-election in one form or another for the rest of my working life.

I'd already decided to give up playing Sunday league football, as union meetings were held on Sunday mornings. My diary tells me that on the first Sunday of 1976, my team, Astra Independent, beat Sunway Blinds 9–2 in the fourth division of the Slough Industrial League, which sums up the loss to football represented by my premature retirement.

While I religiously listed in the back of my diaries the books I'd read, I never catalogued the music I listened to or the records I bought. None the less my musical memory of 1976 is crystal clear as it is entwined with that incredible summer – the hottest since records began.

As luck would have it, this was the year of our very first family holiday. After almost eight years of vacation-less family life the five of us, Judy, Natalie, Emma, Jamie and I, went to a caravan site in Sandy Bay, Devon for a week. Holiday entitlement at the Post Office, both in terms of duration and when it could be taken, was, like progression through the ranks, governed by seniority. Now that I'd been a postman for eight years I was entitled to two weeks' leave in the summer and a week in winter. I still had no chance of taking my summer break in August to coincide with the school holidays. That would take another decade of creeping up the seniority ladder. But at least I now warranted a week in June, a proper summer month. Up until that year my 'summer' allocation had been restricted to May or September because all the popular weeks had been snapped up by men who'd joined the Post Office before me.

We couldn't have picked a more flaming June. We set off for Sandy Bay in our blue Ford Escort just as the long, hot summer of 1976 began. The heatwave would eventually build into one unbroken stretch of sunshine, right through July and August.

Having explored Dartmoor and found our way to Jamaica Inn during the first few days of the holiday, by day four we were ready for the beach. Except that I wasn't. Foolishly, despite Judy's constant warnings as she smothered the kids in suntan lotion, I exposed my fair body to the sun without protection. It demonstrated how stupid I was, for sure, but also how unfamiliar most of us were, in those days, with the power of the sun.

I paid a high price in pain and disfigurement. I felt like a man who'd been condemned to burn at the stake and then reprieved halfway through the execution. For the rest of the holiday I drove my tender carcass to Budleigh Salterton, Drewsteignton and Widecombe, wincing every time the sunlight glanced on my skin through the car window.

The car radio played Abba incessantly, along with Tina Charles, Candi Staton, Billy Ocean and Demis Roussos. But the record that made me reach to turn up the volume was 'The Boys Are Back in Town' by Thin Lizzy. Phil Lynott's narrated vocal, sung over those massive guitar chords, made it the perfect antidote to the tepid tunes commandeering the airwaves that summer. I guess I must still have been heavily under the influence of my great guitar hero, Jeff Beck, because what I liked best about 'The Boys Are Back in Town' was that amazing twin guitar lead on the instrumental break that turned a good record into a great one.

Back at work, being outdoors through that sublime summer made me realise just how much I liked being a delivery postman. So I resigned from the PHG 'acting list' and signed up for the most rural delivery in the entire office – Littleworth Common.

Anyone passing through that part of Buckinghamshire would have seen the local postman with the sleeves of his lightweight summer uniform jacket rolled up, sporting a pair of trendy sunglasses and enjoying to the full what felt like the best job in the world. The only downside was the overtime I still had to do to make ends meet, most of which was based indoors, where the sun didn't shine and air-conditioning had yet to disturb the thick sorting-office atmosphere of heat and dust.

So I also remember 1976 as a summer of Tartan shandies gratefully gulped down at the bar of the Rose and Crown or the Slough Supporters' Club, to which a bunch of us would gravitate on our evening break, like Bedouins heading for an oasis.

Judy's seventh wedding anniversary present to me in July, *20 Golden Greats* by the Beach Boys, was the perfect complement to the kind of day-in, day-out sunshine Californians took for granted but which I had never experienced before, and never have since, come to that. For a brief moment in time, their music and my environment were in true harmony.

It couldn't last for ever, but it was wonderful while it did. The rain finally brought an end to the heatwave in August – just after the government appointed a minister for drought.

1977

Watching the Detectives

PUNK ROCK DID nothing for me. Perhaps I was too old. I completely understood its counter-revolutionary appeal against the musical excesses of the seventies and, if dislike of Emerson, Lake and bloody Palmer had been the required qualification, I'd have been a punk. I hated the sheer pretentiousness and self-indulgence of the prog-rockers (although, paradoxically, Pink Floyd's *Dark Side of the Moon* has always been a favourite album) but punk seemed to go to other extreme, being almost anti-melody as well as claiming to be anti-establishment.

I would sooner have purchased one of those Max Bygraves sing-along albums popular with the older generation at the time than a Sex Pistols LP. All that cod anarchy stuff, contrived to suggest that this was kids doing it for themselves against the odds, was rather spoiled by the fact that the genesis of the movement was in Vivienne Westwood's exclusive fashion emporium in the poshest part of Chelsea.

I only ever saw one punk on the Britwell estate. His name was Richard and he was the seventeen-year-old son of one of our neighbours. Richard suddenly emerged one day wearing lots of studs (including one through his nose), chains hanging off his leather jacket and a pink cockatoo hairstyle. Too well brought up to spit in the street, he would stand self-consciously at the bus stop in front of our house and help old ladies aboard when the bus arrived. Richard never managed to shock anybody and struggled to demonstrate the synthetic outrage expected of him. After a while the chains vanished and he became a New Romantic.

Punk was about as much of a threat to society as Richard was. If it inspired young girls and boys to pick up a guitar, just as skiffle, Elvis and the emergence of the Beatles had done in previous decades, then I suppose it would have had a value but, as the late Mark E. Smith of the Fall once said, 'The great thing about rock 'n' roll is, any idiot can play it. The bad thing about rock 'n' roll is, any idiot can play it.'

As the reign of punk rock was beginning, another was ending. On 17 August, rising early for work, I turned on the radio in the kitchen at 4.30am as usual, to hear the BBC World Service report that Elvis Presley was dead. It was the kind of shocking headline that roots the memory in the spot where the news was heard. It took me a long time to pour the water that had just boiled on to the teabag waiting in my mug as I tried to absorb this information.

Elvis was forty-two, the same age as my mother had been when she died. Linda and I had always felt ambivalent about 'the King' and his music and he had never been prominent in our musical development. Linda was a bigger fan of his British imitators, Cliff Richard and Billy Fury, than of the man himself. But as we reflected over the phone on his demise, we realised that Elvis had always been there in the background. There was the *Old Shep* EP that had brought tears to our eyes as children; his time as a GI, which was always in the news as a backcloth to our formative years; the hit record 'She's Not You' that the teenage Linda had bought for our collection while I was on holiday in Denmark.

Of all Presley's many recordings, there was only one that established itself in my musical subconscious. 'I Feel So Bad' was, I think, released in the UK as a double 'A' side with 'Wild in the Country' in 1961. I suspect that this roaring three minutes of classic rock 'n' roll contained the magic spark that made Presley what he was – a spark that almost vanished in what he became.

When I first heard that saxophone instrumental with Elvis whooping away in the background, it thrilled me to the core. I would have been about eleven or twelve. I played the record over and over again until I was able to transcribe the lyrics. I can remember being totally bemused by some of the vocabulary. I had no idea what a a 'rain check' was, or how a 'grip' could be packed.

Of course, Elvis didn't write that or any of the other songs he sang. That placed him at a disadvantage when the era of Dylan, Brian Wilson and Lennon/McCartney came along. At the time I was being enthralled by the early Beatles stuff, Elvis was having all the excitement managed out of him as 'Colonel' Tom Parker signed him up to a string of awful movies, which improved his bank balance but damaged his credibility.

As I soon discovered, there was now another Elvis on the scene. On hearing '(The Angels Wanna Wear My) Red Shoes' on the radio, I initially assumed Elvis Costello was American.

Such was the impact it had on me that I hotfooted it to my favourite record shop in the Farnham Road to buy it. The only problem was that I didn't know the title of the song or the name of the artist. Either I hadn't managed to catch it on the radio or it had been played by one of those infuriating DJs who failed to name the record they'd just aired because they were too busy projecting their own 'personality' (the cachet of the early Radio 1 DJs had faded for me by now).

I told the helpful assistant that the song was by an American band and tried to reproduce the 'hey, hey' clapping bits, which were what I remembered best about it. Somehow the genius behind the counter, despite having been given misleading information, identified the new Elvis – the one whose forebears hailed from the Wirral peninsula rather than the Mississippi Delta. The debut album from which 'Red Shoes' was taken, *My Aim Is True*, was located and purchased on the spot. And that was the start of my closest and longest affinity with any recording artist.

I suppose that Elvis C. and the other 'new wave' artists I liked, such as Joe Jackson, the La's, Echobelly and Tom Robinson, can be said to have emerged from the punk phenomenon in the sense that punk created the climate that allowed 'independents' to thrive by breaking the command and control of the major record labels.

Costello's label, Stiff Records, promoted many other talented bands that would otherwise have struggled to find an outlet. By contrast, the Sex Pistols, who I would not describe as a talented band, were with EMI, a pillar of the record industry establishment they professed to despise.

I've followed Elvis through everything he's done – the

different genres, various backing bands and numerous collaborations. I've seen him live at every location from the London Palladium to the Sands Leisure Centre in Carlisle and, in forty years of listening to his records and watching him on stage, I have never once been disappointed. If Lonnie Donegan was the musical hero of my childhood, the Beatles of my teens and Bowie of my twenties, Elvis Costello gets the lifetime achievement award. Only four years younger than I am, he seems to have experienced the same kind of musical development, crediting the Beatles as his permanent inspiration.

There is a YouTube video of Costello performing 'Penny Lane' in front of Barack Obama and guests at the White House during the Obama presidency that is the incarnation of this inspiration. Its fruits are also evident in his collaboration with Paul McCartney on two albums, one of his and one of Paul's.

There are other spurious links between Elvis Costello and me besides our mutual adoration of the Fab Four. We were both born in west London and had mothers from Liverpool called Lilian. And I grew up listening to his dad on the radio. Costello's father, Ross MacManus, was a trumpeter and a featured vocalist with the Joe Loss Orchestra, who used to play on those BBC Light Programme music shows, as well as being the resident band at the Hammersmith Palais when I was a kid.

Late in 1977, Elvis Costello released a single that hadn't been on the album. 'Watching the Detectives' remains one of my all-time favourite songs. With its moody Duane Eddy introduction, reggae beat and a lyric that could be better described as a potted film noir screenplay ('She's filing her nails while they're dragging the lake'), this was the song that cemented our unilateral relationship.

~

For my family and me, the whole of 1977 was shrouded in a veil of sadness after the death of my brother-in-law Mike in March. He was thirty-four years old and killed himself, taking a rope into the basement of Henry's Radios, where he'd worked since leaving school.

He had apparently been an alcoholic since his early teens, as my sister had only recently discovered; a 'functioning alcoholic', we'd describe someone with the condition today. Mike was a functioning alcoholic when he came into my life, arriving for a date with Linda at Walmer Road with a Bob Dylan album under his arm; a functioning alcoholic as he enthused me with his love of history, the drawings of Aubrey Beardsley and the books of Ray Bradbury.

A functioning alcoholic when he built me my first amplifier, engineered that weird metal harmonica-holder, bought the tickets for me to see Chuck Berry, paid for a rose tree to be planted at Kensal Rise cemetery to mark the spot where my mother's ashes had been scattered. A functioning alcoholic throughout the entire time we'd known and loved him. A functioning alcoholic until it was too late to escape the demons that tormented him. If he couldn't stop being an alcoholic, he could at least stop functioning. So he did.

Music could offer no solace to Linda, or to me. Nothing could. Kind, gentle, blue-eyed Mike was gone, and for a long while it felt as if all the pleasure in our lives had gone with him.

1978

The Man with the Child in His Eyes

I READ ONLY three books in 1978 but one of them was *War and Peace*, which counts as at least four. I was reading it in February when inflation dropped to single figures (9.9 per cent) for the first time in five years and still reading it in September, when the Labour prime minister, James Callaghan, surprised everybody by announcing that he would not be calling an autumn election.

Tolstoy could have made much of the political drama around that declaration and all that followed. The Conservatives, under the leader of Her Majesty's loyal opposition, Margaret Thatcher, had seen an 11-point poll lead evaporate and, although Callaghan was at the helm of what was effectively a minority government (kept in power by a pact with the Liberals, which had just ended), in September all the signs were that Labour would have won an autumn election.

As a member of the Labour party keen to see my excellent local MP, Joan Lestor, retain her seat and Labour remain in power, I took a deep interest in these machinations.

'Sunny' Jim Callaghan was an avuncular figure who came from a trade-union background and had never gone to university. The only politician ever to hold the four great offices of state (he had been chancellor, foreign secretary and home secretary before becoming prime minister), he would also be the last party leader to have fought in the Second World War.

Callaghan's trade-union credentials couldn't prevent the industrial action that erupted a few months after his announcement and culminated in the 'Winter of Discontent'. It turned the polls against Labour to the extent that even a majority of trade-unionists voted Conservative when the general election was eventually held the following year.

I couldn't even follow these events in the newspaper I'd been buying every day since leaving school in 1965. *The Times* ceased publication on 30 November 1978 due to industrial action and their presses lay dormant for a year.

My union, the Union of Post Office Workers (UPW) never became embroiled in the Winter of Discontent. It had negotiated a reasonable pay deal and was, by temperament and history, loyal to the Labour leadership. In terms of industrial relations we were for peace, but it was war that prevailed, and it put Labour out of power for almost two decades.

～

By now I was the assistant district organiser of the South East No.5 District Council of the UPW. The title was more fulsome than the work it required of me. It was a lay position, the principal function of which was to pay travel expenses to those delegates coming to the monthly District Council meetings from Slough, Reading, Newbury, Maidenhead, Bracknell and Henley-on-Thames.

On my appointment union headquarters provided me with access to some funds to pay out expenses, a typewriter, a large shiny black briefcase and a lapel badge that I never wore (I have an inexplicable aversion to badges of any kind). But the best thing about the job was that I was expected to wear a suit on union business.

I still liked to think of myself as a Mod, having been converted to the cause by a Mod friend of my sister's, who explained their philosophy as 'You may be poor, but don't show poor.' It may have been an ungrammatical motto but, to an impressionable thirteen-year-old, it conveyed the strong message that I was as good as anybody else and should express that in the clothes I wore. It was a lesson that remained embedded in my approach to life.

As so often, Shakespeare captured the sentiment perfectly. In *Hamlet*, Polonius, as part of his inventory of sage advice to his son Laertes, tells him:

> Costly thy habit as thy purse can buy,
> But not express'd in fancy; rich not gaudy;
> For the apparel oft proclaims the man.

When I bought my first suit as a sixteen-year-old I proclaimed myself in Donegal tweed. It was a cheap suit (gaudy, not rich), purchased off the rack at C&A. It made me look like a migraine attack. Things improved sartorially through the seventies, though I did stray from the clean-cut Italianate path of the Mod towards the rougher ground of the Jason

King look: flared trousers, pinched shoulders and wide-peak lapels.

By 1978, there was a Mod revival in full spate, spearheaded by bands like the Jam who mixed the musical and cultural influences of 1960s Mods with elements of the punk genre. True to my roots as an original Mod, I remained in love with the suit, though I'd had enough of Jason. Too old to get down with the kids, but not yet at the age where it would have been difficult to get back up again, I was keen to set my own style, to pre-empt fashion rather than slavishly follow its latest trend. I decided that I could achieve this by wearing a double-breasted suit.

By this point in the 1970s, I would discover, I was so ahead of the times, or perhaps so behind them, that it was impossible to find a double-breasted suit 'off the peg'. Undeterred, I had one tailor-made at Burton's in Slough High Street. That suit remained virtually unworn in my wardrobe. While I had no desire to follow the herd, I found I lacked both the courage and the unconventionality to be a fashion trend-setter, either.

The double-breasted suit made a comeback in the 1980s, albeit in an unappealingly shapeless form. These days, apart from brief appearances in the fashion pages where the style writers attempt to convince the consumer that it is the look of the season, it seems once more to have become the preserve of pea coats, Royal Navy uniforms and our future king. I feel my interest in reviving it beginning to stir again.

~

Kate Bush entered my life in 1978 and has been there ever since. The description 'unique' has been devalued through overuse, but she is one artist for whom it is entirely appropriate.

Kate has divided opinion among music fans ever since the release of her debut single, 'Wuthering Heights', that January. Its originality was beyond dispute but many of my friends couldn't stand it. It had enough supporters to take it to Number 1, in the process making her the first female artist to reach the top spot with one of her own songs, but even those of us who loved the record wondered if she would turn out to be the stereotypical one-hit wonder. As soon as I listened to her first album, *The Kick Inside*, which was in the shops the following month, I knew she wouldn't be.

All the tracks are great and show an astonishing musical maturity for one so young – she was only nineteen when she made that album. But one song made me her devotee for ever. 'The Man with the Child in His Eyes' has a haunting beauty that has defied the years, sounding as fresh and magnificent on its fortieth anniversary as it did when I first heard it.

We Kate Bush fans are not exactly spoiled by the volume of her output. Kate could never be accused of being prolific and has always marched to the beat of her own drum. After the release of her seventh album in 1993 she would drop out of the public eye altogether for twelve years. But what we have been treated to is all the more precious for its rarity.

Linda rang me at Slough sorting office around the time I was eulogising 'Wuthering Heights' to tell me about another record she'd just heard, which she was burning to bring to the attention of her little brother.

A lot had happened to my sister since she'd been widowed at the age of twenty-nine. She had met the man who would become her second husband, Charlie Edwards. The following year, after they married, they would move together to Hockley, Essex, to a house they had built to their own specifications which was big enough for their combined family – they had six children between them.

Essex was where Charlie came from and where he'd sung in clubs and pubs when he was younger. He was a big music fan and had one of those stack hi-fi units that became so popular in the 1980s, from which I remember first hearing Clifford T. Ward, Laura Branigan and the *Bat Out of Hell* album by Meat Loaf ('the artist formerly known as Mince', as one wag dubbed him).

The record Linda was raving about in her phone call was another immortal from 1978. 'Baker Street' by Gerry Rafferty has, in my view, the best introduction to any pop song ever recorded. It tingles and tantalises before bursting into life with Raphael Ravenscroft's magnificent, soaring saxophone riff. Ravenscroft was then a little-known session musician and Rafferty was known to me only as one of the founder members of Stealers Wheel. That record assured the fame of both men.

As Linda bubbled with enthusiasm for 'Baker Street', it was as if we'd suddenly gone back twenty years to the days when we argued at Southam Street about which records to buy. I took my big sister's advice, but with my singles days behind me now, I invested instead in Gerry Rafferty's album, *City to City*.

Whenever Judy and I visited Linda and Charlie it was obvious that she was feeling her way back to happiness after all the trauma she'd suffered before and after Mike's tragic death. She always loved having lots of people around and, after the move to the new house in Hockley, in the organised chaos of a family of eight (which increased to thirteen when we arrived) she was in her element. As well as children of all ages there was a dog to be walked and fish to be fed, although, thanks to me, the latter task was rendered obsolete after our first overnight visit.

Linda and Chas's collection of exotic tropical fish was displayed in two large tanks built into the wall of their living room on either side of the fireplace. As all the bedrooms were full, Judy and I had to sleep on a mattress in the living room. In order to ensure I turned off all the lights, I pulled out the many plugs from their various sockets before retiring. One of them turned out to have been powering the essential air supply for the fish. By morning the entire collection had perished.

This disaster failed to cause a family rift, and Linda continued to ring me with record recommendations. I still consider her tip to buy 'Baker Street' to be one of the best pieces of advice she's ever given me.

1979

Can't Stand Losing You

LIKE MOST BOYS who started smoking young, I gained no pleasure from it initially. I just saw it as a rite of passage, something that was integral to masculinity. My father smoked, as did my mother, in common with every adult in the fifties – or so it seemed. I also thought it would help me to look 'hard' and therefore protect me from being attacked by other boys, who really were hard and were out to do me damage. In other words, I took up smoking for the sake of my health.

Having commenced smoking at twelve, at some stage in my twenties I vowed to give it up by the age of thirty. This was an arbitrary decision based on nothing other than the idea of beginning a new decade of my life nicotine-free. I would make no pronouncements to family or friends, I decided. I'd simply decline when offered a cigarette and hope that nobody would notice I wasn't handing round mine any more. By then I enjoyed smoking. It was comforting, relaxing and reassuring in the sense it gave me of continuity with the past. I liked those small, bonding acts of generosity unique to smokers; the courtesy of passing round what were becoming increasingly expensive little gifts. So I knew that when I eventually gave up it wouldn't be easy.

I didn't smoke many. About ten a day on average, I'd say. As a postman beginning work at around 5am, I had a potentially long smoking day to get through. Fortunately, I could never face a fag early in the morning and the time at which I lit my first cigarette of the day got progressively later until, by the mid-seventies, I wasn't lighting up until midday and sometimes not until the early evening. But despite my low consumption during the week, I could go through a packet of twenty on a night out or a Sunday lunchtime at the British Legion, where I played cards, drank pints and smoked with my male neighbours.

So expense was a factor. The government was in the happy position of increasing the 'purchase tax' on cigarettes at every budget, claiming it as a virtuous disincentive while raking extra revenue into the Treasury vaults. Television advertising of tobacco products wasn't banned until the 1990s and the lucrative sponsorship of sporting events by tobacco companies survived into the next millennium.

But the primary reason for my determination to quit was the harm it could do to my physical wellbeing. My parents' generation were largely unaware of the damage that smoking inflicted, particularly on the heart and lungs. But it was a long time now since smoking had been promoted as beneficial to health. The evidence first uncovered by the British scientists Doll and Hill in the the study they published in the year I was born was now beyond dispute and had been for over twenty years.

There were good reasons, then, for giving up but I also had a motivation. I calculated that if I stopped smoking and re-allocated the money I spent on fags to music, not only would my lungs be healthier but my collection of LPs would be larger.

I was still sixteen months off my self-imposed deadline when I walked into the Post Office canteen on the afternoon of Saturday, 6 January 1979 to collect our three children from the Post Office Christmas party. This event was an unusually egalitarian affair. Throughout the year, the senior managers kept to their own dining facility, with the head postmaster (it was always a man) and his three assistant head postmasters sharing even more exclusive arrangements. These separate enclaves applied horizontally as well as vertically. The clerical grades rarely mixed with the uniformed grades, and 'telecoms' never went anywhere near 'postal'. Except at the Post Office Christmas party, where the children and grandchildren of all staff came together, as did their parents and grandparents, who dropped them off and picked them up afterwards.

Father Christmas (a Post Office supervisor from the Britwell) was still handing out presents when I arrived, so I stood with the other adults on child-collection duty waiting, talking and smoking. Back then there were no restrictions on smoking in the canteen (or 'staff restaurant', as management insisted on calling it), whether it was being used to serve food or doubling up as Santa's grotto.

As I stubbed out my Kensitas, I took a sudden and impromptu decision to make it the last cigarette I would ever smoke. In accordance with my original plan I told nobody at first, not even Judy, who had given up the previous October. I got through my first week of abstinence before acquainting her with my resolution. I took much longer to tell my drinking buddies. I knew that my greatest challenge would be going out for a beer and not smoking. Alcohol seemed to belong with a fag like an envelope belonged with a stamp.

Trying to enjoy one without the other would not be the only hurdle to overcome. I'd seen new quitters subjected to all kinds of subtle inducements to break their willpower: cigarettes offered round with more frequency, smoke blown towards the nicotine-deprived, long, exaggerated sighs of contentment from smokers after every drag and loudly related tales about the rapid weight gain experienced by some other lost soul who had recently been unwise enough to stop smoking.

I was excommunicating myself from the camaraderie around smoking, that tight circle within which friendships flourished. But I was determined that those within the circle wouldn't be aware there was a traitor in their midst until I had become a non-smoker for long enough to be completely resistant to their blandishments. By which time I would be seeing some of the fruits of my decision emerging in my record collection.

I think a packet of twenty cigarettes cost around 59p in 1979. So, on the basis that I was smoking only ten a day, and not counting my increased weekend consumption, I reckoned giving up would save me £2.06 a week. I was actually setting aside £2.50 a week, which I put into an old Black Magic chocolate box. The price of an LP was about £2.99, so the fund wouldn't pay for an album a week, but it would cover three a month.

On my first weekend as a non-smoker, having endured my lonely deprivation for seven days, I felt the need to splash out, so I broke what I came to call the 'tobacco bank' by buying a special reissue of Elton John's double album *Goodbye Yellow Brick Road*. It was pressed in yellow vinyl and cost £4.60.

But the tobacco bank was religiously replenished every week, and thereafter it financed *Armed Forces* by Elvis Costello, Joe Jackson's *I'm the Man* and albums by Supertramp, Squeeze and the Boomtown Rats. Although the Sex Pistols were still around, music had moved firmly into its post-punk phase where the genuine talent that had emerged was leaving most of the dross behind. I loved the Jam, Talking Heads, Tubeway Army, Ian Dury and the Blockheads . . . but most of all I loved the Police.

Those three blond men enchanted me more than Blondie (musically, at least). One of them, Sting, would appear later that year in the film *Quadrophenia* that rode the wave of the Mod revival. He was the perfect choice to play Ace Face, the super Mod. I bought *Regatta de Blanc*, the second Police album, from my tobacco bank and liked it so much that the next week I went out and got their first, *Outlandos d'Amour*.

By now pop music was seeping into the consciousness of Emma and Jamie. Natalie, who hit her teens that October, had long been following the charts. She had gone crazy about *Grease* the previous year, pleading with us to buy her the soundtrack LP by John Travolta and Olivia Newton-John. In January, with the money she'd earned from her paper round, she'd bought her first 7-inch single: 'I Lost My Heart to a Starship Trooper' by Sarah Brightman and Hot Gossip, a sort of disco space song that caught the mood created by films such as *Star Wars* and *Close Encounters of the Third Kind*. The passion for record-buying was passing to a new generation. The entire household heard a lot more music in 1979 as we wore out the stylus on new records financed by my healthier lifestyle.

On holiday that year the five of us sang the Police hit 'Can't Stand Losing You' incessantly as I drove our Hillman Avenger through the narrow lanes of Cornwall. The single had been re-released in June as a follow-up to 'Roxanne'. Eight-year-old Jamie, who loved the band, remarked that ours was a police car. It was officially declared to be his first joke.

1980

In My Life

THE DIARY ENTRY is stark. On Tuesday, 9 December 1980 I wrote: 'John Lennon has been shot dead in New York.'

There it is, recorded amid the other utterly mundane features of that day: the weather ('a milder day today'), office politics in our union branch ('Joe did nothing apart from butt his nose into other people's business all day') and a brief critique of *Ali Baba*, the Lynch Hill School Christmas play ('Emma was the narrator and she did it very well').

The murder had occurred late in the evening of 8 December, New York time, the early hours of the morning in the UK. In an echo of Elvis's death, I heard the news as I tuned into the BBC World Service while filling the kettle and getting ready to go to work. These tasks were completed mechanically as I gleaned further details and tried to make sense of it all through a haze of stunned disbelief and the awareness that I was one of the first on this side of the Atlantic to be feeling it.

The attack had taken place outside John's home in the Dakota apartment building in Manhattan, where a man purporting to be a fan had earlier asked Lennon to sign a copy of *Double Fantasy*, his eagerly awaited new album. John had obliged. That evening, as he was returning from a recording studio, the guy with the signed album shot him.

I recently heard a radio programme about David Halleran, an American of almost exactly the same age as me who had been equally enthralled by the Beatles as a teenager. His favourite was John, whom he'd hoped to meet one day. David went on to study medicine and happened to be the general surgeon on duty at the Roosevelt hospital in New York when staff were alerted to the imminent arrival of a shooting victim in the back of a police car.

The police wouldn't reveal the name of the victim in advance and it wasn't until Dr Halleran was already engaged in trying to restore John's vital signs in the emergency room that he recognised his patient. This lifelong fan was being called upon to try to save the life of his favourite Beatle, holding Lennon's heart in his hand to try to pump it back into life.

Dr Halleran kept his own counsel for over thirty years while two other doctors who hadn't even been in the emergency room at the time claimed the credit for the attempts to keep John Lennon alive. Backed up by other medical staff on duty on the night, and by the account of John's wife Yoko Ono, he spoke up in the end only to correct some of the myths that had grown up around Lennon's death for the sake of historical accuracy.

On that terrible night, thousands of New Yorkers gathered outside the hospital to await news. When it came it was what they feared: despite the heroic efforts of David Halleran and his team, John Lennon was dead.

Today, from my perspective nearly forty years on, it would be easy to overstate the effect of this loss, but if anything, thinking about it now, it's easier still to understate it – to forget the extent of the shock and grief I shared with millions around the world.

Personal bereavement when family members die is obviously the most painful kind and the hardest to bear but, very occasionally, the loss of someone we never knew can produce a collective wave of grief that is as genuine if not as acute. The assassination of John F. Kennedy, the death of Elvis Presley and yes, derided as it often is by the smug and superior, the sudden loss of Princess Diana all fall into this category.

I can't speak for other Beatles fans, but for me it was as if one of the pillars supporting my contented existence had been removed. I obsessed about it day after day through that bleak December. It was ten years since the Beatles had broken up and now they could never get back together again. The death of Lennon was the death of the Beatles.

The album that John had signed for his assassin was his first after five years of virtual hibernation. His first as a solo artist, *John Lennon/Plastic Ono Band*, is in my view his best. I played it again on the day I heard the horrific news. It is almost painfully personal. Opening with 'Mother' and closing with 'My Mummy's Dead', he returns to the theme of the loss of his mother, which he'd explored in Beatles songs such as the superlative 'Julia' on the White Album.

Four tracks in comes 'Working Class Hero', a song I loved to play (inadequately) on my twelve-string. Although it suggests that John wasn't particularly fond of the proletariat (who were 'still fucking peasants' as far as he could see), none the less it fed the myth that he was the most socially deprived Beatle. In fact it was Paul who was the council-house kid. John was raised by his Aunt Mimi in middle-class Woolton. Paul would have to call for him at the back door, stepping on to the lino. The carpet behind the front door was preserved for a better class of visitor. To be fair, none of the Beatles was exactly born with a silver spoon in his mouth. All four of them were steeped in working-class culture and John was unquestionably their leader. The Beatles, like the Quarrymen before them, were his band.

I thought back to the first time I saw the Beatles on TV, with John on the left of the stage taking lead vocal on 'Please Please Me', legs apart, doing little squats as if riding an imaginary motorbike or perhaps a very thin horse. And I remembered how I actually saw him once in person, at such close quarters that I could almost have reached out and touched his leather tunic jacket.

It was at one of those BBC live shows for which Andrew Wiltshire's cameraman neighbour gave us tickets in the midsixties: an early recording of *Not Only . . . But Also*, the BBC2 satirical sketch programme starring Peter Cook and Dudley Moore. It may even have been the pilot in November 1964.

As we took our seats near the front, John Lennon wandered right past us, in his leather jacket, a rollneck sweater and a Bob Dylan cap. With him was the actor Norman Rossington. John was there to read from his second book of nonsense verse, *In His Own Write*, which I'd bought and revered as if it were the *Rubaiyat of Omar Khayyam*.

It was as close as I ever got to a Beatle until I met Paul McCartney forty years later. Paul had always been my favourite, but I would never claim that he wrote better songs than John.

'And Your Bird Can Sing', 'Lucy in the Sky with Diamonds' and 'Strawberry Fields Forever' would settle any argument that John's output wasn't at least as good as Paul's.

Now, following his death, John Lennon's songs were everywhere. Even the august BBC lunchtime news programme *The World at One* on Radio 4 played 'Imagine'. This title track from his second solo album quickly became Lennon's requiem, although I thought of it as more of a dirge. I'd never liked the song. To me it was every bit as twee as McCartney's 'Mull of Kintyre' and twice as pretentious. There were much better songs on that album – 'Jealous Guy', for instance, or the one that came snarling out of the speakers as track six, 'Gimme Some Truth', the magnificently angry antithesis of 'Imagine's' sentimental tosh.

For me, the songs he wrote as a Beatle would always represent John's finest work. The day after his death I confessed to my diary that I couldn't get one of his songs from the White Album out of my head. It was 'Happiness Is a Warm Gun' ('Bang, bang, shoot, shoot').

But this soon gave way to more gentle reflections, on 'I'll Be Back' from the *Hard Day's Night* LP, 'Eight Days a Week' from *Beatles for Sale* and, most powerful of all as an example of what we'd lost, 'In My Life' from *Rubber Soul* – another song that was said to be a lament for his mother.

I played them all as I moped around the house that Christmas inflicting my sorrow on Judy and the kids. Three years later, that sense of loss was rekindled in the greatest musical tribute to John Lennon I've heard. I defy any Beatles fan to listen to Paul Simon's 'The Late Great Johnny Ace', the final track on his *Hearts and Bones* album, without shedding a tear.

1981

Ghost Town

As I LEFT the King's Head in Clapham one warm evening in mid-July 1981, the tension in the summer air was palpable. Shop fronts were boarded up and there were fewer cars than usual driving along Acre Lane, the road that ran alongside the pub and up towards Brixton.

A couple of months earlier, in May, I'd been elected to the Executive Council of my union, by now renamed the Union of Communication Workers to recognise the fact that British Telecom was no longer part of the Post Office. My life had changed profoundly. Although I was still employed as a postman, now that I was a lay member of the governing body of the union I was signed off on special leave for virtually 365 days a year. I was paid by the Post Office but worked for the union.

My Royal Mail uniform had been permanently replaced by a suit and tie and my workplace was no longer the sorting office at Slough but UCW House, the headquarters purpose built for the union in 1933 in Crescent Lane, Clapham, London SW4.

Jim Callaghan's gamble of postponing a general election

until 1979 had failed spectacularly and Britain had its first woman prime minister. As was so often the case throughout the twentieth century, a Labour government had proved to be a brief interlude in a long era of Conservative rule. And although we didn't know it at the time, no institution would suffer more in terms of loss of membership and influence than the trade-union movement.

By 1981 the number of people out of work was at the previously unimaginable level of 2.5 million. Incredibly, it would rise to beyond 3 million as Labour remained unable to dislodge the Tories. In Brixton, in south-west London, the unemployment figure was higher than average, and among ethnic minorities it was higher still. Around 55 per cent of the Afro-Caribbean youth of Brixton were out of work. The area, which had been getting more decrepit for years, was blighted by poor housing and soaring crime rates. As the Scarman Report was to conclude later in the year, there had been 'disproportionate and indiscriminate use of "stop and search" against the black community' by the Metropolitan Police, supplemented by the notorious Special Patrol Group, the unit dedicated to combating serious public disorder and related crime.

In January, at a house party in New Cross, three or four miles east of Brixton, thirteen black youngsters had died in a fire and the belief that it had been started deliberately by white supremacists, while unsubstantiated, had become entrenched among local black people. The community was outraged by what they saw as indifference on the part of the authorities and the press and some 15,000 protesters marched in central London calling for action.

This toxic mix of deprivation, suspicion, grievance and

discrimination culminated in the Brixton riots that had erupted between 10 and 12 April and involved as many as five thousand people. Now, in July, the country had seen riots breaking out in Southall in west London, Toxteth (Liverpool), Handsworth (Birmingham), Chapeltown (Leeds) and Moss Side (Manchester). Brixton, inevitably another potential flash-point, remained eerily quiet but volatile, like dry tinder needing only a spark to burst into flames.

I'd gone to the King's Head with some of the staff from UCW House who lived nearby, many in Brixton itself. We all left the pub after one drink. Nobody wanted to be going home after the sun went down, when the risk of trouble rose dramati-cally. While my workmates were heading into the heart of the tension I was driving away from it, west along the M4, which took me out of London and home to the Britwell estate. As I drove, the car radio played the hit that had been at Number 1 for weeks: 'Ghost Town' by the Specials.

Rarely has a pop record so accurately reflected the mood of the moment. This was astute social observation with a reggae beat. The Specials' hypnotic song, written by the band's key-board player, Jerry Dammers, and released on the 2 Tone label, fully deserved all the accolades it was to receive. Two-tone, the music genre that fused ska and reggae with echoes of punk, orig-inated in the Specials' home town of Coventry. Characterised by mixed-race bands and black-and-white garb teamed with pork pie hats, it was a musical metaphor for racial harmony.

There were no riots in Slough. While the town itself was racially diverse, the Britwell was almost totally populated by white working-class families. Labour had held the constituency (which went under the splendid title of Eton and Slough) in

1979 but Joan Lestor, our wonderful MP, would be defeated at the next election.

Although the high levels of unemployment affected people of all ethnicities, Slough fared better than many towns owing to its location in the prosperous Thames Valley. Its trading estate had been generating jobs since the 1930s. So my thirty-mile journey from Clapham took me into a much more serene landscape, free of the pervasive atmosphere of hopelessness and despair that was emanating from Brixton and Toxteth.

That year was a strange mixture of riots and royalty. It was only a couple of weeks after the worst of the unrest that Prince Charles married Lady Diana Spencer and we all got a day off to celebrate. It was hoped that the occasion would boost public morale, if only for a day or two. The extent of the government's concern that the wedding would be marred by violence in the streets was revealed only thirty years later with the release of official files that detailed how Mrs Thatcher wanted to arm the police and equip them with water cannon, tear gas and rubber bullets (plans resisted by senior police officers).

It is interesting that, just as in the twenty-first century blame for unrest is often laid at the door of social media, in 1981 the government appeared to be pointing the finger at the influence of television. As it turned out, calm was restored by the day of the royal wedding, but only just: a second wave of rioting in Toxteth ended only the day before.

∼

My three children were becoming more and more interested in music and the artists who made it. Natalie was devoted to

Haircut 100, Emma to Bucks Fizz (who won the Eurovision Song Contest in 1981 with 'Making Your Mind Up'), and ten-year-old Jamie, who'd begun to apply himself seriously to the acoustic guitar we'd bought him a few years earlier, still idolised the Police. He also had a special fondness for the Kim Wilde single 'Kids in America'.

And we all liked Adam and the Ants, whose songs and videos were such fun. By now, with technology enabling video recording and editing to be done quickly and cheaply, the pop video was beginning to play an important part in the marketing of music and becoming a significant factor in the success of any record. Gone were the days of artists simply miming to their hits on *Top of the Pops*. This was the year when the video channel MTV was launched in the States, heralding the era of round-the-clock music on television.

Adam and the Ants were among the artists to capitalise on the growing popularity of the promotional video by producing creative little films to enhance their appeal. The video for their single 'Prince Charming', in which Diana Dors – the 1950s starlet once touted as Britain's answer to Marilyn Monroe and something of a national institution – appeared as the Fairy Godmother, was the best thing on telly for a while. Not that I saw much TV. My new life was peripatetic. When I wasn't driving up to Clapham, I was touring the country trying to sort out disputes and tutoring at the union's educational weekend schools.

In August my new role took me abroad for the first time since that childhood holiday in Denmark for London's inner-city kids. It wasn't the first time I'd been on a plane – I'd completed my maiden flight, or flights, only two months earlier aboard the 4.30pm 'shuttle' from Heathrow to Manchester and a tiny twenty-seater onward to Dundee, where there had been a disagreement to settle.

Now, at the dubiously youthful age of thirty-one, I was leading a UCW delegation to the International Confederation of Free Trade Unions (ICFTU) Youth Conference in Seville. If I was expecting to live the high life in Spain, I was soon disappointed.

On our arrival, in searing heat, our delegation of eight was shown to a tent that would be our home for ten days. Inside was nothing but grass which grew rough and spiky. There was no groundsheet, or indeed anything else, in the tent, apart from an ants' nest in the middle. We eventually got hold of some polythene sheets to sleep on. A thousand delegates from all over the world were to live in similar accommodation in this tent city, with rudimentary toilet facilities and about fifty cold-water showers, at the hottest time of the year, when temperatures were topping 100 degrees Fahrenheit.

Within a week I was in the camp hospital with suspected dysentery. An outbreak spreading through the camp was so severe that the West German authorities sent their own doctors to Seville to treat their delegation and make sure they didn't bring the disease home with them.

Fortunately, it transpired that I didn't have dysentery, but I was very poorly all the same. Never had I been so pleased to be ill. It meant I was able to spend the last few days of the conference in the relative luxury of the camp hospital rather than sweltering in the sparsely equipped tent. From my bed on the top floor of the four-storey medical centre, I could hear the music from the nightly open-air concerts, provided by a different country every evening. There was Spanish dancing, South American musical theatre and traditional Indian music, all very highbrow and cultural.

On the last night it was evidently the turn of the Brits. All I could hear from what sounded like a combined choir of British, Irish and Australian piss artists was a ragged, impromptu performance of Joe Dolce's 'Shaddap You Face'.

It wasn't my favourite record of the year but the song title would certainly have been been the first to spring to mind as a suitable response if anyone ever again asked me to attend a ICFTU World Youth Conference.

1982

Allentown

I STILL HAVE the first compact audio cassette (CAC) I ever bought. It's nothing to look at. A squat, stunted little thing that could never match for style or beauty the product it was designed to replace.

In the 1980s the desire to enjoy music any time, anywhere led to the demise of vinyl and the satisfyingly substantial LPs that were cherished for more than the music they contained. The problem was that they didn't fit into a Sony Walkman or a combination car radio and cassette-player.

It would be a few years before I had a car that had a built-in cassette-player, but in 1982 we did update our domestic music-listening arrangements, replacing Judy's old black English Electric record-player with a 'Hifi Stereo Sound System' that had two box speakers, a record turntable and a cassette device with settings for 'play' and 'record'. The days of the reel-to-reel tape-recorder were over. Tapes were now reduced in size, sealed within a plastic case barely longer than a packet of cigarettes, and considerably thinner. There were blank ones for recording on and others, with album cover artwork reprinted on a bit of cardboard slotted into the case, masquerading as records.

Having acquired the sound system, I went out and bought that first CAC: Billy Joel's *The Nylon Curtain*. I wish I could play it now. There is a connection between the music and the object on which it is stored. Just as those shellac 78s, and the Bachelors' album bought for Lily which she didn't live to hear, had a significance of their own, so can the humble cassette. The physical shape and feel of it, the ritual of taking it out of its plastic case and snapping it into the cassette-player, peering myopically at the tiny type of the 'sleeve notes' reduced to fit the small format, are all somehow bound up with the love of the music it holds, the memories associated with the early enjoyment of listening to it and, in the case of my copy of *The Nylon Curtain*, the novelty of this new mode of playing it. But the age of the cassette tape has, in its turn, passed and while it's still possible to buy the necessary equipment, like double-breasted suits in the 1970s, it is extremely difficult to find.

The opening track of *The Nylon Curtain* is a belter. 'Allentown' was as profound a comment on the decline of America's rust belt as anything Bruce Springsteen ever wrote. And 'Goodnight Saigon' is an eloquent statement on US involvement in Vietnam. Yet Billy Joel has never been considered cool enough to be an authentic social commentator. Such are the mysteries of public perception.

We chose our hi-fi sound system from a Brian Mills catalogue, for which one of our neighbours was an emissary. The big catalogue companies had agents across the council estates of Britain who formed an almost entirely female amateur sales force. They received a modest commission on items purchased and relied on friends and neighbours to boost their earnings. It was only through the 'keepers of the catalogue' that orders could be placed. The flimsy pink form on which they were recorded would be dispatched and the item delivered to your door a few weeks later, if not by the 'next-day delivery' we expect now, at least within a month. Usually.

The contraption was assembled on our sideboard down at the dining-room end of the through lounge and we thought it was one of the most exciting cultural developments of our married life. It came with an audio jack into which you could plug a microphone or headphones, and later in the year I invested in a set of headphones, which revolutionised the whole business of listening to records in a small council house with thin walls and three kids.

Our house was semi-detached by virtue of its position at the end of the terrace. We got on well with our friendly neighbours but the wall we shared wasn't built to be soundproof and they had small children too, so we were constantly concerned about disturbing each other's tranquillity. When we played records the volume had to be restrained. But the most immediate problem wasn't the comfort of the neighbours. In a long living room with a telly at one end and a 'Hifi Stereo Sound System' at the other, there was a constant struggle between whether to watch or listen. The telly usually won.

As the children had small bedrooms (Judy and I had moved into the back bedroom when Jamie was little, enabling us to divide the larger front bedroom into two for the kids), and the house had no central heating, everyone tended to congregate in that long room with its Rayburn fireplace and large dining table upon which games could be played and homework completed.

So buying those headphones was as good as building on another room. Now any one of us could opt out of whatever else was going on, don the headphones, turn the volume up as high as we liked and escape into our personal choice of music.

It wasn't a shared experience, but there again, it rarely had been before. And if we wanted to sit down and listen to a record together, we still could. More often than not my desire to play a record had been trumped by the kids' desire to watch *Fame*, *Dallas* or *Blake's Seven*.

I no longer needed the motivation of the tobacco bank. I remained a non-smoking record collector, and I collected a lot of them in 1982: *English Settlement* by XTC, *Night and Day* by Joe Jackson, *Avalon* by Roxy Music, *1999* by Prince, *Love Over Gold* by Dire Straits. I bought records by the well-known (the Jam, Tom Petty, Squeeze) and the more obscure (the Cocteau Twins, Todd Rundgren and an American artist by the name of Marshall Crenshaw, whose eponymous debut album was bursting with great pop songs but who never made the big time).

I suppose the acknowledged album of the year has to have been Michael Jackson's *Thriller*, which is the biggest-selling record of all time, or so I am told. But it didn't thrill me, and I am not among the many millions who have bought it, despite some mild pressure from Natalie, who was by now sixteen and considered me, at twice her age, to be hopelessly out of touch with youth culture.

My album of the year, and one of the best in rock history as far as I am concerned (irrespective of how many it has sold) was *Imperial Bedroom* by Elvis Costello. Listening to it through those headphones was an exquisite experience. There were elements of tracks such as 'The Long Honeymoon', 'Pidgin English' and 'You Little Fool' that would have been indiscernible without them.

Imperial Bedroom is one of the many albums that I now own in triplicate. First I bought the LP, then I got it on cassette so that I could play it in the car (a listening experience almost as good as the headphones for purity of sound) and finally, in the early 1990s, I acquired the compact disc. Now, despite ever more sophisticated methods of listening to music being developed, it is my original vinyl version that is coveted. One thing is for sure: the compact audio cassette will not be making a comeback. But I have kept mine. They are small chunks of musical history and they take up little space in proportion to all the memories they hold. Like old foreign coins, they will always be around in a corner of a drawer somewhere in whatever house I am living in.

~

I went to my first Labour party conference in 1982, having been elected as a UCW delegate. Following Labour's defeat in 1979 the party had fallen into a frenzy of infighting and self-loathing, with the main thrust of the hostility being directed against previous Labour governments. This 'culture of betrayal' was driven by a sect whose members had always despised Labour and the democratic socialism it represented. Now this outfit, the Revolutionary Socialist League, was infiltrating our ranks through its newspaper, *Militant*.

The local party in Slough wasn't as factionalised as those in many other constituencies but there were enough militants there to turn our meetings into endurance tests. Obsessed with the rules and standing orders, they imposed their stern and humourless presence to such an extent that party events became increasingly disorderly and unpleasant.

The troublemakers were predominantly middle-class men in their thirties whose declared aim was greater membership involvement. In reality this meant ensuring that their small clique could run the show. They were like religious zealots demanding that anybody who rejected the true faith be denounced as traitors. Those Labour party members who had a life to lead and no time to waste in long, unproductive, bad-tempered meetings soon stopped attending, leaving the clique in greater control.

These people may have made inroads in local constituency parties, but they had yet to capture the castle. That the Labour leadership was still beyond their reach didn't prevent the 1982 conference in Blackpool being a rancorous affair. Every point of procedure was contested, with a line of shouty people queuing to take the rostrum and deliver little two-minute harangues on obscure procedural matters.

Our delegation of postmen and telephonists, dressed smartly, as we believed we should be when representing our members, felt out of place in a conference hall where half the delegates were in denim or dungarees covered in badges bearing uncompromising slogans proselytising the causes they'd come to advance.

In the wider political landscape, the Falklands War had begun in April, as the Tories struggled in the opinion polls, and ended in June with Mrs Thatcher riding the wave of patriotic pride generated by a military victory over the Argentinians, who had tried to invade a British Crown colony. And a third force had entered British politics after four prominent Labour MPs left the party to form the Social Democratic Party (SDP), which had quickly formed an alliance with the Liberals.

So far had the stock of my divided party fallen in the eyes of the electorate that back in April it had been the new SDP–Liberal Alliance that had been ahead of the Tories in the polls, not Labour.

On the Thursday of the conference Joan Lestor invited me to have lunch with her and the Slough delegates. Also present was her predecessor as Labour MP for the town, Fenner Brockway. Fenner was the grand old man of British socialism. He was ninety-four and now sat in the House of Lords as Baron Brockway of Eton and Slough. A founding member of CND, he'd been a Labour rebel himself on many occasions, but the latest upheaval, he declared to me, was more uncomradely than any of the clashes he'd seen in the past. The Labour party had always been a coalition of idealism and pragmatism but had managed the tensions between those two strands with mutual respect and tolerance. Now he feared those values were being undermined.

He told me he had only ever had two heroes: Keir Hardie, who'd adopted Brockway as his political protégé, and Rosa Luxemburg, the Polish Marxist feminist who was murdered by paramilitaries during a political uprising in Germany in the 1920s. Fenner said to the table at large: 'If only Lenin had listened to Rosa, the whole course of history would have changed.'

The diners fell silent. How do you engage in conversation about left-wing politics with a man who has been personally acquainted with Keir Hardie, Rosa Luxemburg and Vladimir Lenin?

~

Back in the real world, which the Labour party seemed to have temporarily vacated, my friend Andrew Wiltshire had become a victim of the rising unemployment statistics.

He had been working for a drugs company that had spent months training him to be a salesman, only to discard him along with half the sales force. It was the first time either of us had experienced redundancy in the twenty years since we'd entered the world of work. When Andrew rang me to convey the bad news I could tell he was upset and worried about the future. We agreed to have one of our regular get-togethers and soon I was on my way to Tring with Judy and the kids.

It was a Sunday, the day that Andrew usually played drums in a jazz band at the Crown in Berkhamsted, a few miles down the road from Tring. By now our eldest children were old enough to take charge of our amalgamated tribe at Andrew's house while Judy, Ann and I went off to see Andrew in action and enjoy a pub lunch.

He had reassembled a drum kit in the years since the Great Theft from the Fourth Feathers. Jazz had always been his first love and, as he'd given up any serious musical ambitions, playing in this pub gave him the opportunity to do something he was extremely good at just for fun.

The band played in a room over the pub that was all bare boards and massive beams. It gradually began to fill up and by 1pm it was jam-packed with jazz enthusiasts from all over the county. You could tell they were jazz enthusiasts because they wore corduroy and drank real ale.

I watched Andrew with an almost fraternal pride. He was such an outstanding drummer and it was a pleasure to see him lost in the enjoyment of each long piece the band played. This was the perfect antidote to the gloom that had descended on him with the redundancy notice.

It wasn't long before I discerned that there were a couple of celebrities in the audience. John Williams was one of the world's most renowned classical guitarists. It was his solo recording of Stanley Myers' 'Cavatina' that had become a worldwide hit record after it was used as the theme to the Oscar-winning film *The Deer Hunter* in 1978. And here he was on this Sunday lunchtime, sitting a few feet away from Andrew Wiltshire, the brilliant former drummer of the Area.

By this time John was with the fusion group Sky. He was accompanied by the other celebrity – his partner Sue Cook, the *Nationwide* TV presenter. Apparently, the couple lived nearby. I reflected on Andrew's strange ability to gravitate into the orbit of the famous. The boy who had become friendly with Pat Boone and almost joined the Mindbenders was now playing a lunchtime jazz session in front of one of the greatest musicians in the world and one of the most familiar faces on British television at the time.

Watching Andrew play reignited my desire to make music as well as listen to it. I still played guitar for my own enjoyment, although the piano had gone, almost by accident. It was getting very old and went out of tune quickly, so when I saw an advert in the local paper for a company in Windsor who offered to collect unwanted pianos, fully restore them and then offer them back at a reasonable price, it seemed like a good solution.

As things turned out, the first part of the deal was completed but not the second. Off went our battered old piano, with a promise from the driver who collected it to ring me when it was fully refurbished. No call ever came. It seemed I'd been had, but I'd failed to keep the advert with the phone number on it and, with no means of tracking the piano down, there wasn't much I could do about it. The space left in our through lounge was very soon filled with other things. Perhaps that white piano found its way to someone else's living room and is still sitting there today. Who knows?

My Eko twelve-string still hung from the wall on its picture hook and I'd written a fair number of songs over the years that sounded OK to me. But my working schedule was too unpredictable and involved too much travel to allow me even to think of joining a local band. So how could my yearning to be involved in pop music again be satisfied?

As we drove back to Slough that Sunday evening, an idea suddenly seized me. It was one of those lightbulb moments beloved of cartoonists. I would place a blank cassette tape into our 'sound system', record some of my songs and send the tape to Elvis Costello at the address printed on the sleeve of *Imperial Bedroom*. Only he would have the impeccable taste to appreciate my *oeuvre* and the contacts at Stiff Records to nurture this raw talent.

I waited until the house was empty one Saturday morning before arranging myself on a dining-room chair next to the sound system, guitar on my knee, microphone positioned in front of me on its little tripod, and rushing quickly through six of my songs – the best of the hundred or so I'd written over a twenty-year period. The crème de la crème of my songwriting genius.

I wrote a nice letter to Elvis, listing the song titles along with my name and address, and sent it off by first-class post in November 1982.

I'm still waiting to hear back.

Everyday I Write the Book

MUSIC DIDN'T END for me in 1982. Of course it didn't. But that cassette I sent to Elvis Costello was my last attempt of any kind to fulfil my boyhood ambition to be a rock 'n' roll star. My other adolescent aspiration was to be a writer, and things have gone rather better for me in that respect.

It's early in 2018 and, as the Beast from the East roars its defiance against the coming of spring, I'm finishing this account of my twenty-five-year quest for rock stardom. It has been fifty-four years since my English teacher, Mr Carlen, encouraged me to send off those stories and poems to the publishers whose addresses, on his advice, I gleaned from *The Writers' and Artists' Yearbook*. I kept the inevitable rejection slips for a long while but I was too young and optimistic to feel that they in any way represented a door slammed in my face, especially since Mr Carlen had told me that every successful writer received enough rejection slips early in their careers to paper their walls. I kept them as certificates of my endeavours. And in 2013 I made sure that Mr Carlen was present at the launch party for my first book.

I never intended to return to writing but I did. I always intended to return to playing music but I never have.

A news item catches my eye. The Rolling Stones are to make their first UK tour in twelve years. They will fill huge stadiums with devoted fans of all ages, although it's safe to predict that most will be from My Generation.

The Rolling Stones were formed fifty-six years ago, in 1962. It is impossible to imagine that, in 1957, when this book begins, a bunch of popular musicians who had been stars since 1901 could have been about to embark on a sell-out tour. Yet that would have been the equivalent longevity.

It was two years into their existence that I first saw the band live, at the Wimbledon Palais (which, the last time I passed it, had been converted to a furniture store, the Stones having out-lived most of the venues they played in their early days). Colin James was with me that evening in 1964 to witness the early hysteria that surrounded the band.

Mick Jagger was chased off the stage by some over-enthusiastic girls and, as he sought the sanctuary of the dressing rooms, with the fans in hot pursuit, he brushed past Colin and me. He rushed through a door leading off the dance hall but one of the girls managed to squeeze through after him and follow him up the stairs. A few minutes later we saw her legs dangling almost dir-ectly above us as the ceiling gave way (I distinctly remember that she was wearing tights). I don't think any harm was done, except to her modesty.

The Stones keep rolling on, linking me and millions more to a childhood that was also the infancy of rock 'n' roll. I've never believed that the music of my teens is all that's worth listening to; quite the opposite. I've always felt that the greatest period in pop history is the current one: new artists and bands emerge, the choice becomes wider, the genre richer. Today I listen to Arcade

Fire, Laura Marlin, St Vincent, Everything Everything, the 1975, the Arctic Monkeys, Courtney Barnett, the Blue Aeroplanes, John Grant, Villagers, Regina Spektor ... I'm introduced to amazing new artists on a regular basis. But the genesis of all of them, every single one, lies back in the 1950s and 1960s with Elvis Presley, Chuck Berry and, of course, the Beatles.

The evolution of pop music is not a linear progression, or the replacement of one kind of music with another, but an accumulation of all the talent, experimentation and influences that have contributed to it since its inception.

Sometimes it feels more circular than linear. Who would have foreseen, in 1973, that Slade's 'Merry Xmas Everybody' would still be blaring out of shops, pubs and parties every December? Or, even more improbably, in 1969, the year humankind first set foot on the moon, that a half-century on David Bowie's voice would be posthumously calling to Major Tom on an infinite loop in space? It is now issuing from the speakers aboard, of all things, a red Tesla Roadster car in a projected billion-year elliptical orbit of Mars. It is said that nothing can be heard in space. What a shame Bowie couldn't have written 'Is There Sound in Space?' to go alongside 'Is There Life on Mars?'

Down on Earth, vinyl and CDs continue to co-exist with iTunes and Spotify, and the government has never succeeded in completely eradicating pirate radio stations, in spite of periodic clampdowns. None have had the huge audiences or influence of the pirate ships of the 1960s, of course. Still, there have been waves of land-based, urban stations that reflect the musical tastes and community interests of an increasingly diverse Britain. All that was needed in the 1970s and 1980s was a decent cassette-player and the roof of a tower block to transmit from. Today there are fewer pirate stations, probably about 150 of them around the country, mostly in London. Research suggests their listeners feel that licensed broadcasters do not provide enough of what a younger public want, or air enough new music. The more things change, the more they stay the same, as they say.

After 1982 I became even more immersed in the Labour movement, from which I emerged only in 2017. In the eleven years I spent as a government minister I never picked up my guitar once. As soon as the electorate dispensed with our services in 2010 I went to a music shop not far from Parliament and bought a Yamaha acoustic six-string. I began to play again, the fingertips on my left hand gradually becoming callused as they reacquainted themselves with the strings and frets.

Then a guy in Edinburgh contacted me, having read about me once playing a Höfner Verithin. He had one for sale and drove down to Hull to show it to me. We met in the Holiday Inn on the marina on a crisp autumn day and exchanged small-talk before he opened the heavy black guitar case that rested across the arms of a wooden chair in the deserted hotel lounge. As the hinged lid lifted, so did my heart. I felt sure that this was the very guitar I'd first fallen in love with when I gazed at it through the window of that music shop in Wardour Street all those years ago: the beautiful, cherry-red Höfner purchased for £35 and cruelly taken from me on that night of skulduggery in an Islington pub.

I had no way of proving it, but very few Verithins were made with this particular combination of distinctive features and none at all, I believe, after 1963. In a strong light, a serial number was visible through one of the Venetian cutaways, but as I didn't know the number of the one that was stolen, I had nothing to check it against. I did not, I hasten to say, suspect my new friend from Edinburgh of being involved in the theft. The fact that he wouldn't have been born when the robbery took place seemed a reasonable alibi. Whatever adventures my beloved Höfner had experienced, it had obviously been well looked after by its subsequent owners. I coughed up the asking price of £800, the transaction was completed and it was at last back where it belonged.

And so I have (probably) got the guitar I bought in 1965; the weather has been as close to the dreadful winter of 1962–3 as I've seen since; the Stones are touring; students in Paris are protesting and the UK will soon be out of the European Community, just as we were back then. It may well be time to put the band back together again.

Acknowledgements

My grateful thanks to:

My wife Carolyn, to whom this book is dedicated, for her constant encouragement and endless practical support.

My literary agent, Clare Alexander of Aitken Alexander, who came up with the idea of a music memoir.

Doug Young, who did so much for me and for many other authors at Transworld.

Larry Finlay, Patsy Irwin and all the wonderful people at Transworld.

Caroline North McIlvanney, still the finest editor in the business.

My sister, Linda Edwards, who always helps to jog my memory on aspects of our shared childhood.

My Liverpudlian friend Billy Hayes, who gave me some valuable information about Beatles songs.

My media agent, Andrew Wilson of Cloud9 management, who first set these chapters of my life to music for a public event.

Kall Kwik printers in Hull, for all their assistance with the photographs.

Picture Acknowledgements

All photographs have been kindly supplied by the author except those listed below. Every effort has been made to trace copyright holders; those overlooked are invited to get in touch with the publishers.

Page 2, top, Lonnie Donegan and his band: © United Archives GmbH/Alamy.

Page 3, top, Chuck Berry, *Johnny B. Good* record sleeve: © Chess records.

Page 4, bottom, Denmark Street with Margo and the Marvettes: © PA/PA Archive/PA Images.

Page 6, bottom, the Beatles at Abbey Road Studios: © David Magnus/Rex/Shutterstock.

Page 8, top, Kate Bush: © Pictorial Press Ltd/Alamy.

Page 8, middle, Elvis Costello and the Attractions: © Estate of Keith Morris/Redferns/Getty Images.

Page 8, bottom, Noah and the Whale with Alan Johnson, Theresa May and Nick Robinson on *The Andrew Marr Show*: © Jeff Overs/BBC.

Song Acknowledgements

Lyrics on p.5 from 'True Love' written by Cole Porter

Lyrics on p.20 from 'American Pie' written by Don McLean

Lyrics on p.77 from 'Old Shep' written by Red Foley and Arthur Williams

Lyrics on p.92 from 'Summer in the City' written by John Sebastian, Mark Sebastian and Steve Boone

Lyrics on p.110 from 'San Francisco' written by John Phillips

Lyrics on p.111 from 'Whiter Shade of Pale' written by Gary Brooker, Keith Reid and Matthew Fisher

Lyrics on p.118 from 'All or Nothing' written by Steve Marriott and Ronnie Lane

Lyrics on p.118 from 'Wild Thing' written by Chip Taylor

Lyrics on p.128 from 'Words' written by Barry, Robin and Maurice Gibb

Lyrics on p.141 from 'Space Oddity' written by David Bowie

Lyrics on p.144 from 'When Father Papered the Parlour' written by R. P. Weston and F. J. Barnes

Lyrics on p.147 from 'The End' written by Lennon–McCartney

Lyrics on p.166 from 'Suffragette City' written by David Bowie

SONG ACKNOWLEDGEMENTS

Lyrics on p.171 from 'Merry Xmas Everybody' written by Noddy Holder and Jim Lea

Lyrics on p.185 from 'Bohemian Rhapsody' written by Freddie Mercury

Lyrics on p.196–7 from 'Watching the Detectives' written by Elvis Costello

Lyrics on p.213 from 'Working Class Hero' written by John Lennon

Lyrics on p.215 from 'Happiness is a Warm Gun' written by Lennon–McCartney

Index

INDEX

Index

INDEX

INDEX

INDEX

Index

INDEX

Index

Alan Johnson's life as a paperback writer

From the condemned slums of Southam Street in West London to the corridors of power in Westminster, Alan Johnson's multi-award-winning memoirs chart an extraordinary journey, almost unimaginable in today's Britain.

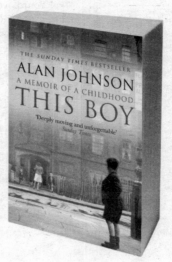

'Beautifully observed, humorous, moving, uplifting: told with a dry, self-deprecating wit and not a trace of self-pity'
OBSERVER

Played out against the background of a community living in condemned housing in London's Notting Hill pre-gentrification, this is the story of two remarkable women. Alan Johnson's mother Lily battled poor health, poverty, domestic violence and loneliness to try to ensure a better life for her children. And his sister, Linda, who took on an adult's burden of responsibility and fought to keep the family together when she herself was still only a child.

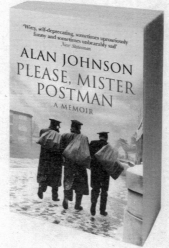

'Beautifully written . . . vividly observed'
DAILY MAIL

In July 1969, while the Rolling Stones played a free concert in Hyde Park, Alan Johnson left London to start a new life as a postman in Slough. It was a job that involved long working days and endless overtime, but there were compensations – the crafty fag snatched in a country lane, the farmer's wife offering him breakfast and the mysterious lady who appeared at her window every morning – topless. But as life appeared to be settling down and his career takes off, his close-knit family is struck once again by tragedy.

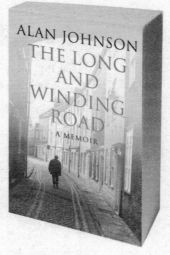

'Johnson writes with his usual warmth, wit and honesty'
SUNDAY TIMES

Alan Johnson's negotiating skills and charisma as a trade
union leader brought him to the attention of Tony Blair.
Selected to stand in the constituency of Hull West and Hessle,
he entered Parliament as an MP after Labour's landslide
election victory in May 1997. Supporting his
constituents – the Hull trawler-men and their families
in their search for justice – comes more naturally to him
than do the Byzantine complexities of Parliamentary
procedure. But he succeeds nonetheless, rising
through the ministerial ranks to the office of
Home Secretary in 2009.